The
Lucent
Library
of
Historical
Eras

The Roman Army

Instrument
of Power

Other titles in the Lucent Library of Historical Eras include:

Elizabeth I and Her Court
Great Elizabethan Playwrights
A History of Elizabethan Theater
Life in Elizabethan London
Arts, Leisure, and Entertainment: Life of the Ancient Romans
From Founding to Fall: A History of Rome
Influential Figures of Ancient Rome
Words of the Ancient Romans: Primary Sources

The Lucent Library of Historical Eras

The Roman Army
Instrument of Power

Don Nardo

LUCENT BOOKS®

THOMSON

GALE

San Diego • Detroit • New York • San Francisco • Cleveland • New Haven, Conn. • Waterville, Maine • London • Munich

© 2004 by Lucent Books. Lucent Books is an imprint of The Gale Group, Inc.,
a division of Thomson Learning, Inc.

Lucent Books® and Thomson Learning™ are trademarks used herein under license.

For more information, contact
Lucent Books
27500 Drake Rd.
Farmington Hills, MI 48331-3535
Or you can visit our Internet site at http://www.gale.com

LIBRARY OF CONGRESS CATALOGING-IN-PUBLICATION DATA

Nardo, Don, 1947–
    The Roman army: instrument of power / by Don Nardo.
        v. cm. — (The Lucent library of historical eras. Ancient Rome)
Includes bibliographical references and index.
Contents: Rome's early enemies and expansion—Undisputed masters of Italy—Rome
against Carthage: round one—Rome Carthage: round two—Roman armies overrun
Greece—Julius Caesar conquers Gaul—Rome's early imperial conquests—Epilogue: the
Roman army's decline.
    ISBN 1-59018.316.9
    1. Rome—History, Military—Juvenile literature. 2. Rome—Army—Juvenile literature.
[1. Rome—History, Military. 2. Rome—Army.] I. Title. II. Series.
    DG89.N39 2004
    937—dc21

                                                                    2003005757

Printed in the United States of America

Contents

Foreword

Looking back from the vantage point of the present, history can be viewed as a myriad of intertwining roads paved by human events. Some paths stand out—broad highways whose mileposts, even from a distance of centuries, are clear. The events that propelled the rise to power of Germany's Third Reich, its role in World War II, and its eventual demise, for example, are well defined and documented.

Other roads are less distinct, their route sometimes hidden from view. Modern legislatures may have developed from old tribal councils, for example, but the links between them are indistinct in places, open to discussion and interpretation.

The architecture of civilization—law, religion, art, science, and government—as well as the more everyday aspects of our culture—what we eat, what we wear—all developed along the historical roads and byways. In that progression can be traced every facet of modern life.

A broad look back along these roads reveals that many paths—though of vastly different character—seem to converge at a few critical junctions. These intersec-

tions are those great historical eras that echo over the long, steady course of human history, extending beyond the past and into the present.

These epic periods of time are the focus of Lucent's Library of Historical Eras. They shine through the mists of history like beacons, illuminated by a burst of creativity that propels events forward—so bright that we, from thousands of years away, can clearly see the chain of events leading to the present.

Each Lucent Library of Historical Eras consists of a set of books that highlight various aspects of these major eras. For example, the Elizabethan England library features volumes on Queen Elizabeth I and her court, Elizabethan theater, the great playwrights, and everyday life in Elizabethan London.

The mini-library approach allows for the division of each era into its most significant and most interesting parts and the exploration of those parts in depth. Also, social and cultural trends as well as illustrative documents and eyewitness accounts can be prominently featured in individual volumes.

Lucent's Library of Historical Eras presents a wealth of information to young readers. The lively narrative, fully documented primary and secondary source quotations, maps, photographs, sidebars, and annotated bibliographies serve as launching points for class discussion and further research.

In studying the great historical eras, students also develop a better understanding of our own times. What we learn from the past and how we apply it in the present may shape the future and may determine whether our era will be a guiding light to those traveling future roads.

Introduction:
Empires Won by Force of Arms

The concept of a nation using its army as an instrument of power, especially to conquer other nations, is nothing new. History is replete with examples. The first-known large-scale conquest occurred between 2400 and 2200 B.C., when a Mesopotamian people, the Akkadians, attacked their neighbors in what is now Iraq and created an empire. There followed numerous other empires won by force of arms, among them the Babylonian, Assyrian, Hittite, Egyptian, Persian, Macedonian (Greek), and Roman, to name only the more famous ones. None of these empires would have been possible without large, well-equipped armies and entrenched, revered military institutions.

It is not surprising, therefore, that the most successful and long-lived of these ancient empires also possessed the most efficient and widely feared army. Indeed, ancient Rome was, and remains, renowned for the organization, discipline, and effective use of its army. Much has already been written about the Roman military and its exploits. But the subject is immense and historically important. One simply cannot understand and appreciate Rome's contribution to Western civilization without a careful examination of its conquests and the military machine that made them possible. As historian Michael Grant puts it, Rome's conquests

> exercised profoundly far-reaching effects on all subsequent history. For this was one of the greatest and most formidable armies that has ever existed. Moreover, it was the conditions the Roman army created which enabled Rome to bring into effect its vast, peculiar, and specific contributions to civilization, which have to such an extent made our modern life, for better or worse, what it is. The army, therefore, which produced these far-reaching and permanent results deserves continuing investigation and analysis.[1]

A Stubborn, Resilient People

The rise of Rome to a position of power over the Mediterranean world was therefore much dependent on and a direct result of its development of a highly effective army. However, two essential points must be kept in mind when examining said conquests and army. First, Rome's rise to a position of dominance was neither quick nor easy. It was instead "a slow, painstaking process fraught with many setbacks," military historian Peter Connolly points out. "It was this slow process, accompanied by long periods of consolidation, which was the main reason for the longevity of the subsequent Roman Empire."[2]

Indeed, early Rome took on its rivals one by one over many centuries. It first gained mastery over its local Italian neighborhood and then the whole Italian peninsula. Next, it conquered the western sphere of the Mediterranean, followed by the east-

ern sphere. Finally, it captured Gaul (what is now France), Egypt, Britain, and parts of central Europe. Many victories contributed to this successful expansion; yet the Romans suffered a number of debilitating defeats as well, some so severe that they would have utterly destroyed most other nations. To their credit, the Romans were an amazingly stubborn and resilient people who were loathe to admit defeat. And time after time they bounced back from the brink of doom and won resounding victories.

Not One but Many Armies

The other essential point to remember about Rome's military successes over the centuries is that to speak of the "Roman army" is potentially misleading. Just as the

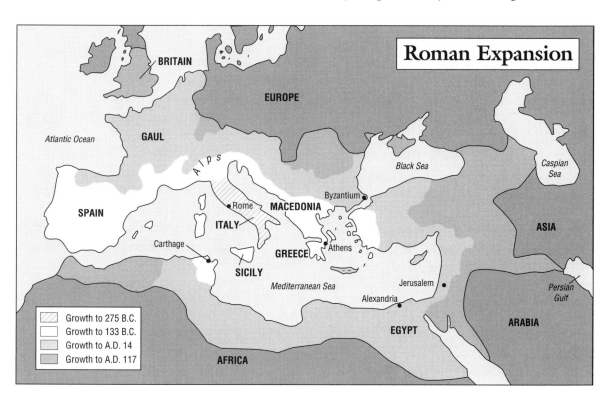

Roman Expansion

Growth to 275 B.C.
Growth to 133 B.C.
Growth to A.D. 14
Growth to A.D. 117

The most basic individual unit of Roman power was the legionary, a truly formidable warrior.

first that army was a part-time citizen militia whose members fought with thrusting spears and went home after fighting one or two battles. Later military reforms drastically altered this situation. Completely reorganized, the army became more flexible, emphasized the use of throwing spears and swords, and began taking the soldiers far from home for long periods. Later still, the army underwent new bouts of reorganization that emphasized different weapons and tactics and the changing strategies of the commanders and emperors. Eventually, the army admitted more and more foreigners into its ranks and became increasingly less disciplined and effective, until, in the twilight of Roman civilization, it could no longer adequately defend the realm.

There was never a single, typical, or characteristic Roman army, therefore, but many, often distinctly different Roman armies. The appearance, techniques, and effectiveness of each depended on the age in which it existed. And each must be considered, in its turn, in telling the momentous story of how Rome, which began as a small Italian village, managed to conquer the known world.

character of Roman government and society changed enormously over the span of some twelve centuries, so did the army. At

Rome's Early Enemies and Expansion

Modern historians are unsure when Rome's first conquest took place. This is partly because Rome is a very ancient town whose origins and early history are shrouded in the mists of time. The most likely scenario for the city's founding is that a number of small villages grew atop a group of low hills occupying the future site of Rome, near a bend in the Tiber River a few miles inland from Italy's western coast. Archaeological evidence confirms that at least some of these villages were flourishing by 1000 B.C. It is possible that they fought periodically over grazing or water rights; but these conflicts cannot be described as Roman wars or conquests since Rome technically did not yet exist.

Only when the villages coalesced into a single central town, or city-state, did the so-called eternal city spring into being. The famous story that a noble youth named Romulus erected the city from scratch is almost certainly pure legend. The traditional date for this event, as computed by later Roman scholars, was 753 B.C. It is more likely that what the later Romans commemorated, unknowingly, was actually the time when the original villages became unified. Romulus, whom legend touted as Rome's first king, may have been the first or perhaps the most accomplished early leader of the unified city-state (assuming he was indeed a real person, which remains unproven).

During the two or so centuries that followed, Rome continued to be ruled by kings. According to legend, there were seven—Romulus, Numa Pompilius, Tullus Hostilius, Ancus Marcius, Tarquinius Priscus, Servius Tullius, and Tarquinius Superbus (or "Tarquin the Proud"). However, the first few may not have been real, and there may well have been other kings whose names have been forgotten. Then, in about 509 B.C. (or perhaps a few years later), the Romans abolished the Monarchy and established the Republic, which featured a legislature—the Senate—and a number of elected officials, including two supreme administrator-generals, the consuls.

Throughout the Monarchy and the first century of the Republic, a period of more than three hundred years, Rome fought numerous wars and significantly expanded its territory. By later ancient standards, and certainly by modern ones, these wars and conquests were small. And all took place in a relatively tiny patch of western Italy sandwiched between the sea and the Apennine Mountains. All of the enemies the Roman army faced during this period—the Sabines, Etruscans, Volsci, Aequi, and various Latins—were close neighbors whose territories eventually became part of the central Roman heartland.

Etruscans and Sabines

The pattern that Rome's early wars and conquests would follow was in large part dictated by the way its potentially hostile neighbors were situated. In effect, they surrounded the tiny Roman city-state, hemming it in on all sides. To the west, northwest, and north stretched Etruria (today called Tuscany), homeland of the Etruscans, an ancient Italian people who were considerably more culturally advanced than the early Romans. There was no overriding Etruscan "nation"; rather, the region was divided into a dozen or more powerful city-states, each centered on a well-fortified town and each viewing itself as a separate nation. One of the strongest of these city-states, Veii, was destined to become a thorn in Rome's side, mainly because it was, as Michael Grant puts it, "intolerably close." Indeed only about twelve miles separated the two cities. "This extremely short distance between the two places," Grant continues,

meant that neither could ever feel safe from the other. Veii was powerful and its geological position extremely strong. It was situated on a steep, sheer plateau and surrounded on three sides by a moat of running water, including, beneath the eastern end of the citadel, the River Cremera . . . which went on to flow into the Tiber five miles north of Rome. . . . Given such extreme proximity [closeness] competing demands [of Rome and Veii] for markets, land, and coastal salt were bound to lead to serious clashes and had probably done so as early as the seventh century B.C. For the Tiber was a highway that had to be controlled either by Veii or by Rome; in the long run, no compromise was possible.[3]

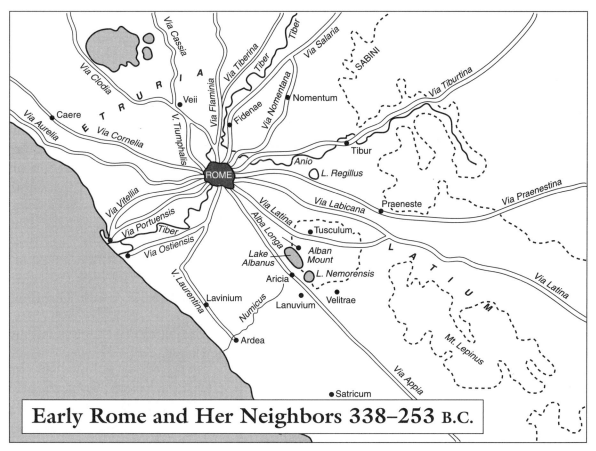

Early Rome and Her Neighbors 338–253 B.C.

Northeast of Rome lived the Sabines (Sabini in Latin), who spoke Oscan, a tongue related to but distinct from Latin. Some of the Sabine towns, including Cures, were very close to Rome. And it is possible that a group of Sabines actually inhabited some of Rome's Seven Hills as late as the eighth century B.C. This would inevitably have led to rivalry with the Roman villages on the other local hills.

In fact, one of the most famous of all Roman legends tells how the early Romans faced a shortage of women. So King Romulus invited the Sabines of neighboring towns to a festival and then had his men steal the Sabine women, who soon became Roman wives and mothers. According to the great first-century B.C. Roman historian Livy, the Sabine men eventually returned armed to the teeth, and a major battle took place on the flat ground between the Palatine and Capitoline hills. Suddenly, though, the women intervened. "With loosened hair and rent garments," Livy wrote,

they braved the flying spears and thrust their way in a body between the em-battled armies. They parted the angry

Romulus Steals the Sabine Women

This excerpt from Livy's great history (quoted in Livy: The Early History of Rome*) describes the famous capture of the Sabine women by Rome's early male inhabitants.*

On the appointed day [of a festival to which the Romans had invited the neighboring Sabines], crowds flocked to Rome, partly, no doubt, out of sheer curiosity to see the new town. . . . All the Sabines were there . . . with their wives and children. . . . Then the great moment came; the show began, and nobody had eyes or thought for anything else. This was the Romans' opportunity. At a given signal, all the able-bodied men burst through the crowd and seized the young women. Most of the girls were the prize of whoever got hold of them first, but a few conspicuously handsome ones had been previously marked down for leading [Romans], and these were brought to their houses by special gangs. . . . By this act of violence, the fun of the festival broke up in panic. The girls' unfortunate parents made good their escape, not without bitter comments on the treachery of their hosts. The young women were no less indignant and as full of foreboding for the future.

combatants; they besought their fathers on the one side, their husbands on the other, to spare themselves the curse of shedding kindred blood. . . . The effect of the appeal was immediate and profound. Silence fell and not a man moved. A moment later the rival captains stepped forward to conclude a peace.[4]

The treaty provided that the two peoples combine as one. And, thereafter, Romulus and the Sabine king, Titus Tatius, ruled Rome jointly. Though this story smacks heavily of fable, it may be based on a real war in Rome's dim past, one in which it defeated a Sabine city and signed a treaty with its king.

Latins and Hill Peoples

Roman legend also recalled early wars against Rome's southern neighbors, the Latins. The Romans were themselves Latins, of course. Rome was situated on the northern rim of the fertile plain of Latium, where most of the Latin city-states were clustered.

In perhaps the most famous early legendary war between Rome and another Latin city, the Romans struggled against the Alba Longa. Both sides suffered heavily, losing many fine soldiers. Moreover, the Roman and Alban kings worried that their common enemy, the Etruscans, might try to take advantage of their growing weakness and attack both Rome and Alba Longa. So the two leaders called a truce, and, in Livy's words, the Alban king declared:

> We should admit that our two nations, close neighbors and blood relations as we are, have a deeper reason for going to war: I mean ambition and the love of power. . . . But what I would suggest to you . . . is this. You know the strength of the Etruscans, who threaten to encircle us . . . and you know it even better than we, as you are closer to them. They are strong on land, and at sea very strong indeed. . . . Do not forget . . . that they will be watching us, ready, when we have worn each other out, to attack us both, victor and vanquished alike. . . . We should be able to find a better solution [to our differences].[5]

So the two kings agreed that the war between them would be decided by a fight among six men—three champions from each side. The three Romans came from the noble Horatii family; the three Albans were members of the equally respected Curiatii family. The two armies gathered around to watch the battle, which ended with the last of the Horatii slaying all three of his Alban opponents. According to Livy:

In French artist Jacques-Louis David's great painting, the Sabine women throw themselves between the two armies in an attempt to end the war.

The cheering ranks of the Roman army . . . welcomed back their champion. The two sides then buried their dead, a common task but performed with very different feelings by victors and vanquished. Alba was subject now to her Roman mistress.[6]

The Alban king had spoken of the Etruscans threatening "to encircle" the Romans and other Latins. Two other peoples began to do just that during the latter years of the Roman Monarchy. The Volsci and Aequi originally inhabited the heavily forested western slopes of the Apennine Mountains in central Italy. These fierce tribal peoples wanted to exploit the rich farmlands of Latium as well as gain access to the sea (to take advantage of maritime trade); they eventually descended from the hills into the southern reaches of Latium, creating a direct threat to the Latin cities.

Early Roman Military Organization

These many successful military campaigns that the early Romans launched against their neighbors make it clear that Rome had a formidable and effective army. An important question is how this army was organized. Also, how did it fight on the battlefield? Unfortunately, very little solid evidence has survived to answer these questions completely. Yet based on snippets of ancient literary texts and a few scattered archaeological finds of armor and weapons, modern scholars have pieced together the following plausible scenario.

The king was the commander in chief of the army. But he needed officers to help him manage the troops, so unit commanders emerged, each known as a tribune, or "tribal officer." Rome originally had three traditional tribes, so there were three tribunes. Each commanded one thousand men, all of whom were patricians, landowners, and well-to-do men who could afford to own weapons and armor, which were very expensive at that time. That brought the total number of infantrymen, or foot soldiers, to three thousand. The Romans called this force a legion. The legion also broke down into thirty units of one hundred men each, called centuries.

Supporting the legion was a cavalry force made up of three hundred well-to-do men called *equites,* or "knights." Livy and other later Roman scholars assumed that these early knights were armed men who fought on horseback. However, most modern historians believe they were an elite group of citizens who rode their steeds to the battlefield and then dismounted and fought on foot. All of these soldiers, whether part of the legion or knights, were part-time soldiers, a militia that assembled in an emergency, fought a battle, and then went home.

Adoption of the Phalanx

This situation changed significantly sometime in the early-to-mid sixth century B.C. The Roman army underwent an important reorganization as it adopted a mili-

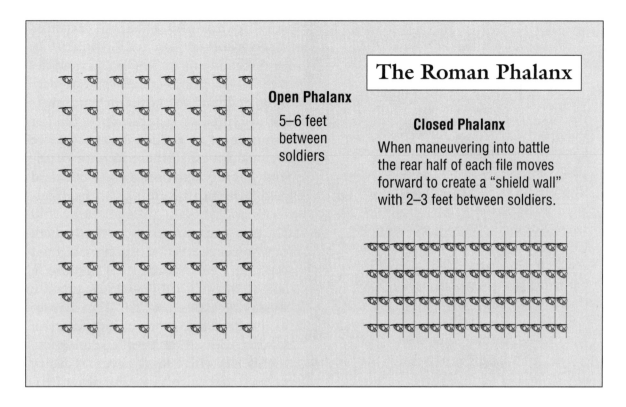

The Roman Phalanx

Open Phalanx

5–6 feet between soldiers

Closed Phalanx

When maneuvering into battle the rear half of each file moves forward to create a "shield wall" with 2–3 feet between soldiers.

tary system that had recently originated in Greece. It was based on heavily armored infantry soldiers called hoplites, who wore metal cuirasses, helmets, and greaves (lower-leg protectors).

Greek hoplites formed a battlefield unit known as the phalanx, consisting of ranks (lines) of soldiers, one standing behind the other. The average depth was eight ranks, but sometimes a commander called for more than eight or as few as three or four. When fully arrayed, the phalanx presented a wall of upright shields and forward-pointing spears to the enemy. This created not only a formidable defensive barrier but also an offensive formation having tremendous and potentially deadly forward momentum. As the phalanx made contact with the soldiers in the opposing army, the hoplites in the front rank jabbed their spears at the enemy; meanwhile, the hoplites in the rear ranks shoved at their comrades' backs, pushing them with great force toward the enemy.

Typically, the hoplites, all upper-class men who could afford the armor and weapons, were accompanied by supporters who carried the hoplites' armor and provisions to the battlefield. These supporters also helped wounded hoplites off the field and chased down and killed fleeing enemy soldiers who had discarded their own armor in an effort to run faster. The supporters were poorer men who

A Fleeing Hoplite

In hoplite warfare, warriors who were defeated and running for their lives often discarded their heavy armor, including their shields. The following short poem (translated in Kenneth J. Atchity's *Classical Greek Reader*) by a seventh-century B.C. Greek, Archilochus, was famous across the Mediterranean world: "Well, what if some barbaric Thracian glories in the perfect shield I left under a bush? I was sorry to leave it—but I saved my skin. Does it matter? O hell, I'll buy a better one!"

wore little or no armor, carried wooden shields, and wielded javelins (throwing spears), swords, daggers, axes, and various farm implements.

The techniques of phalanx warfare reached central Italy in the early seventh century B.C. A number of Greek cities had recently been founded in southern Italy, and their new and highly effective fighting style immediately caught on with some local Italian peoples. Among the first were the Etruscans. And within a generation, all of the city-states of central Italy, including Rome, had adopted the phalanx.

The adoption of the phalanx by the Roman army was probably part of a major program of military reforms called the Servian reforms. Another part consisted of a census of the male population. Once a list of the men's names, status, and net worth had been compiled, the populace was divided into six classes on the basis of wealth (expressed in *asses*, an *as* being a common unit of Roman currency). The army was also divided into groups based directly on and matching these social classes. According to Livy:

> Of those whose property was rated at a capital value of 100,000 *asses* or more, 80 centuries were formed, 40 of "seniors" and 40 of "juniors." This whole group was known as the First Class. The seniors were for civil defense, the juniors for service in the field. All were required to equip themselves with helmet, round shield, greaves, and breastplate. The defensive armor was of bronze. Their weapons of offense were the sword and spear.[7]

Thus, of the eight thousand men making up the first class, half of them, probably men over the age of forty-five or fifty, performed the "civil defense" duty of guarding the city in an emergency. The other four thousand men were the hoplites who manned the phalanx. Livy goes on to explain that the second, third, fourth, and fifth classes were made up of progressively lighter-armed troops. Their job was to support the phalanx on the battlefield. Finally, members of the sixth class—Rome's poorest citizens—did not have to serve in the army at all. Somewhat later, during the fifth century B.C., another reform raised the number of hoplites in the phalanx from four thousand to six thousand.

Roman Conquests in the Fifth Century B.C.

The Romans' adoption of hoplite warfare was one of many examples of their ability to borrow ideas from other peoples and make them fit their own needs. Their phalanx, combined with their native courage and tenacity, brought them much success on the battlefield during the century following the founding of the Republic. And that success often translated into the Roman state acquiring more territory and/or increasing its influence in Italian affairs.

The first major test came in a clash with the Latin League. This military alliance of the leading Latin towns, including Rome, had formed during the late seventh century to help protect the members against outside threats. Alba Longa had originally led the league, but after defeating the Albans in battle, the Romans assumed this role. In about 500 B.C., likely fearing Roman expansion, the other members of the league began to oppose Rome. In a great battle fought in 496 B.C. at Lake Regillus, about fifteen miles southeast of Rome, the Roman phalanx went up against a large army of Latins. In Livy's account, the Roman line momentarily faltered and fell back. But then the Roman commander, Aulus Postumius,

issued an order to the picked troops who were serving as his personal guard to cut down every Roman soldier

whom they saw trying to save his own skin. The measure was successful; threatened simultaneously from front and rear, the Romans turned to face the enemy, and the line [of hoplites] was reconstituted. . . . The Latins wavered, and then broke.[8]

After the battle, the Romans and Latins signed a treaty that was significant for two reasons. First, its provisions implied that Rome was equal in status and influence with the rest of the league. As Grant points out, this meant that, by force of arms, Rome had already become "sufficiently

The typical armor and weapons of central Italy in the sixth century B.C.

Roman troops prepare to besiege the Etruscan fortress-town of Veii. The Romans and Etruscans fought each other for generations.

strong to be recognized as the equal of the principal Latin cities combined."[9]

Second, the treaty gave Rome needed allies against increasing incursions of the Volsci and Aequi in the years to come. The Romans fought major battles against the Volsci in 482 and 468 B.C. and against the Aequi in 465, 458, and 455. After that, the two hill peoples combined forces against the Romans and Latins. Finally, in 431 B.C., at Mount Algidus in Latium, a Roman army crushed the enemy, inflicting heavy losses and selling all the surviving Volsci and Aequi into slavery.

Even as these intermittent wars were raging, Rome had to face another formidable foe on its northern flank, namely the Etruscan stronghold of Veii. Cattle raids and other small-scale hostile incidents escalated over time into open war-

fare. To protect Rome, the members of a prominent Roman family, the Fabii, built a fort just seven miles from Veii. But in about 477 B.C., the people of Veii attacked the fort and its garrison of about three hundred Romans, killing all but one of them.

Many battles between the two peoples ensued that year and in the following several years. Finally, after a long siege, Rome captured Veii in 396 B.C. The victors destroyed much of the once impressive city and incorporated its surrounding lands into the Roman city-state, nearly doubling its size. At the time, the Romans must have seen this expansion as an awesome achievement. They could scarcely imagine that the territory they now controlled would pale in comparison to the vast domains their immediate descendants would win by the sword.

Chapter

2

Undisputed Masters of Italy

For a few years following their sack of the Etruscan city of Veii, the Romans must have felt a great deal of pride. Their once tiny city-state was now many times larger than it had been under the early kings. And the Romans had earned a reputation for toughness and resilience throughout Italy and beyond. The realm's military deserved much of the credit for this enhanced status, partly because the army was well equipped and also because it had fought often over the preceding decades. Frequent campaigning had ensured that there was always a core of battle-hardened veterans in the ranks.

That situation evidently changed after the fall of Veii. For about five or six years, the Romans fought no major battles, and the military ranks began to swell with young new recruits. According to the first-century A.D. Greek biographer Plutarch, "Most of them [were] raw soldiers, and such as had never handled a weapon before."[10] This state of affairs could not have come at a worse time. In about 390 B.C. Rome suddenly faced a formidable enemy from an unexpected quarter. The Gauls, a branch of the Celts, descended from central Europe and delivered the Roman army a shattering defeat.

Though disastrous, in a way this event may actually have helped Rome in the long run. The shaken Romans completely overhauled their military, and over time the new system they developed became the most efficient and lethal in the known world.

Rome's conquests continued, therefore. And only a little more than a century after its embarrassing defeat, it had managed to absorb nearly all of Italy.

The Dark Day of Allia

The Romans lost their first encounter with the Gauls mainly because they did not know their enemy. Rome and its neighbors had heard of the arrival of strangers in extreme northern Italy in about 400 B.C. The Gauls quickly overran the Po Valley, the region lying immediately south of the Alps. But for the Romans, these events seemed far away. No one in central Italy had ever seen a Gallic army in action.

Then a large force of Gauls marched southward through Etruria, began sacking Etruscan cities, and threatened Roman territory. Historians Arthur Boak and William Sinnegin describe these unique intruders:

> Drunkenness and love of strife were their characteristic vices, war and oratory their passions. . . . Their chief weapons were long, two-edged swords of soft iron. . . . For defense they carried small wicker shields. Their armies were undisciplined mobs, greedy for plunder. . . . Brave to the point of recklessness, they were formidable warriors, and the ferocity of their first assault inspired terror even in the ranks of veteran armies.[11]

Indeed, the Roman force that marched out to meet the Gauls on July 18, 390 B.C., was one of the armies that succumbed to this "terror." The Romans may have numbered as many as thirty thousand to forty thousand. Of these, six thousand probably manned the phalanx, the army's core unit, while the rest acted as supporters and reserves. The problem, as Plutarch pointed out, was that most of these troops were inexperienced.

When they reached the Allia River (a few miles north of Rome), they were confronted by tens of thousands

The Gauls drive the inexperienced Roman recruits into the Allia River in one of Rome's most embarrassing defeats.

of fearsome-looking Gauls, some wearing animal skins, others nearly naked, and all long-haired and adorned with war paint. These "wild men," as the young Romans saw them, immediately launched a screaming charge. The attackers drove a company of Roman reserves off the hill on which they had been posted; the fleeing reserves then ran right into the Roman phalanx, creating disorder and confusion. The Gauls were not far behind, and the men in the phalanx wasted no time in retreating in what Plutarch calls "a disgraceful" manner, "devoid of order and discipline." The phalanx's "left wing was immediately driven into the river, and there destroyed. The right [wing] had less damage,"[12] and some of its members fled to the nearby ruins of Veii, hoping to find shelter.

Three days after the battle, the victors entered and sacked Rome, which had by this time been largely evacuated. Soon afterward, the Gauls departed. According to the second-century B.C. Greek historian Polybius, they left because word had come that their own territory in the far north had been invaded by a neighboring tribe. Another account claims that the Romans bribed the intruders to leave by giving them a large sum of gold. In any case, in later centuries the anniversary of the humiliating defeat, July 18, was called the dark "Day of Allia," an unlucky date on the Roman calendar.

Major Military Reforms

The defeat at Allia may have had a much more crucial repercussion than mere shame and humiliation, however. Roman leaders likely concluded that the battle had been lost because the young recruits had panicked. Yet even if they had held their ground, they would in all likelihood have been overwhelmed anyway. What is certain is that at some point after the encounter with the Gauls, the Romans showed their military wisdom by recognizing the inherent weaknesses of the phalanx. They realized that it was too rigid since it demanded that all of its members remain fixed in their ranks, regardless of the situation. So a large, free-moving mass of enemy troops, like the Gauls, could too easily outflank, or move around the sides of the formation.

The only acceptable course seemed to be to abandon the phalanx entirely and adopt new battle formations and tactics. Accordingly, over the course of several years, a group of military reformers created a new Roman army. In the new Roman military system, a legion no longer consisted of a single, monolithic phalanx but instead broke down into several smaller units on the battlefield. These units were called maniples. Each maniple could act independently of the others and also could combine with them in various ways, which made the army as a whole considerably more flexible. The reformers dispensed with the circular hoplite shield. In its place, they installed a slightly larger oval-shaped (later rectangular) shield called the *scutum*, which they felt afforded a soldier better protection.

Finally, some (and later all) of the newly equipped Roman legionaries gave up their thrusting spears for shorter throwing spears, or *pila*. This innovation made the new military system much more flexible and effective. In the phalanx, the hoplites could not use their spears to engage the enemy soldiers until the two armies made contact. By contrast, the new legionaries could throw their *pila* at long range and damage the enemy *before* the armies made contact. Then, when the opposing lines did engage, each legionary could draw his thrusting sword (the *gladius*) and hack away.

Organization of the Manipular Army

Because the new Roman military system emphasized maniples as basic tactical units, it became known as the "manipular system." Once this new army was fully developed, its superior offensive and defensive features virtually ensured the success of future Roman conquests and expansion. Among the system's strongest points was its flexible organization, which exploited the strengths of various kinds of fighters. It also gave these fighters excellent, often precision training and drilling. And it gave strategic thought to the many possible situations that might arise in battle, including the need for an ordered retreat.

No detailed descriptions of an early Roman manipular army and its maneuvers have survived. The first such description was that of the Greek historian Polybius, about two centuries later. (Some changes

Livy on the Panic at Allia

Livy's version of the battle at Allia is more detailed than Plutarch's. Here, from Aubrey de Sélincourt's translation in Livy: The Early History of Rome, *is part of Livy's account.*

In the lines of the legionaries-officers and men alike—there was no trace of the old Roman manhood. They fled in panic, so blinded by everything but saving their skins that, in spite of the fact that the Tiber lay in their way, most of them tried to get to Veii, once an enemy town, instead of making for their own homes in Rome. . . . The main body of the army, at the first sound of the Gallic war-cry . . . hardly waited even to see their strange enemy from the ends of the earth; they made no attempt at resistance . . . but fled before they had lost a single man. . . . Near the bank of the river there was a terrible slaughter; the whole left wing of the army had gone that way and had flung away their arms in the desperate hope of getting over. Many could not swim and many others in their exhausted state were dragged under . . . and drowned.

in the system must have occurred by his day, but it is likely that they were fairly minor.) According to Polybius, when arrayed on the battlefield the army consisted of several separate lines or groupings, each featuring a different sort of fighter. The front line was the only one not organized into maniples. Usually a few ranks deep, it was a solid mass of light-armed skirmishers known as *velites*, very young men who wore no armor and carried javelins and a shield.

Behind the *velites* stood the main part of the army, the infantrymen, deployed in three long lines, one behind the other. Each line was made up of maniples, with spaces separating one maniple from another. The maniples and spaces of the three lines were staggered so that there was open space on all sides of each maniple, overall producing a sort of checkerboard effect. (This pattern resembled the dots representing the number five on a dice cube, which the Romans called a *quincunx*; so they gave the battlefield formation the same name.)

Of these three lines of maniples, the first was made up of the *hastati*, young men with a minimum of experience but having a great deal of vigor and endurance. Polybius says that each *hastatus* carried a *scutum*, along with "a sword which is worn on the right thigh . . . two throwing spears, a bronze helmet, and greaves," and wore a cuirass "which is placed in front of the heart, and called a heart-protector (*pectorale*)."[13] Each maniple of *hastati* (and each maniple in the other two lines) was composed of two centuries, one positioned behind the other. (By this time, a century contained eighty rather than one hundred men.)

The second line of maniples, positioned directly behind the *hastati*, was manned by soldiers called *principes*. Experienced fighters in the prime of life (probably aged twenty-five to thirty), they carried the same armor and weapons as the *hastati*. The third and final line of maniples featured a fourth type of soldier— the *triarii*, older veterans who lacked the physical endurance of the others but had more experience. According to Polybius, the *triarii* carried the same armor and weapons as the *hastati* and *principes*, with one exception. Instead of two *pila*, each of the *triarii* wielded a thrusting spear almost exactly like the one used by the hoplites in the old phalanx.

Classic Manipular Tactics

This organization into four lines, one of skirmishers and three of maniples, allowed Roman commanders a considerable amount of flexibility in executing tactics of attack and defense. Many diverse maneuvers were possible. But most were variations on a basic offensive approach in which the four kinds of fighters engaged the enemy one at a time. As the Romans advanced and the enemy line drew close enough, the *velites* opened the battle by charging forward and hurling their javelins. The intent was to try to damage or at least hamper the enemy army before the Roman legionaries launched their main attack.

Having thrown their javelins, the *velites* turned, quickly retreated through the open spaces in the three lines of maniples, and reformed their line in the rear, behind the *triarii*. Meanwhile, after the last of the skirmishers had made it past the *hastati* in the front line, the rear centuries of *hastati* swiftly moved from behind the front centuries and filled the gaps in the line. This formidable solid bank of infantry now charged forward, the men shouting fiercely in unison in an attempt to frighten the enemy. At a distance of about one hundred feet, the *hastati* hurled their light javelins and a few seconds later followed with their heavy ones. Then they drew their swords, rushed forward, and crashed into the enemy ranks with as much impact as possible.

Sometimes the *hastati*'s charge hurt and/or demoralized the enemy enough to force its retreat, giving the Romans an easy victory. Other times this first line of legionaries found it difficult to make any headway or suffered more than light casualties. If this happened, the Roman commander signaled for the *hastati* to retreat. Like the *velites* had, they hurried through the gaps separating the remaining maniples and stood behind the *triarii*. Meanwhile, just as the *hastati* had done earlier, the *principes* formed a solid line and charged the enemy, who now had to face a force of fresh soldiers with even more battle experience than the *hastati*.

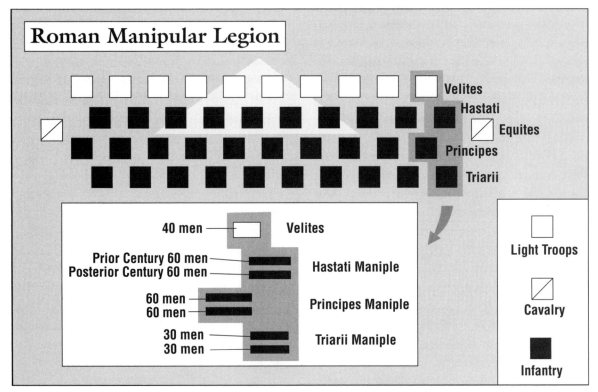

Roman Manipular Legion

Velites
Hastati
Equites
Principes
Triarii

40 men — Velites
Prior Century 60 men — Hastati Maniple
Posterior Century 60 men —
60 men — Principes Maniple
60 men —
30 men — Triarii Maniple
30 men —

Light Troops
Cavalry
Infantry

The Roman Manipular Tactic

■ Triarii	▢ Hastati
▣ Principes	···· Velites

Stage 1. The army assembles with the *velites* forming a frontal screen. The maniples (each composed of two centuries) of *hastati*, *principes*, and *triarii* are arranged in a checkerboard pattern behind them. The battle begins with the *velites* running forward and hurling their javelins at the enemy.

Stage 2. At a given signal, the *velites* retreat through the gaps among the maniples and re-form their line in the rear. Meanwhile, the posterior centuries of the maniples of *hastati* move forward and fill the gaps in their line, forming a solid front. The *hastati* then charge and engage the enemy.

Stage 3. If the enemy is able to resist the *hastati*'s assault, or if the *hastati* begin to suffer serious losses, a trumpet blast orders them to retreat, and they move back through the gaps among the maniples. The centuries of the maniples of *principes* now form a solid line, as the *hastati* did earlier, and launch their own charge on the opposing army.

Stage 4. If the *principes* are unable to secure a victory, they retreat through the gaps among the maniples of *triarii* and fill in the gaps among the maniples of *hastati*. The *hastati*, who have had a chance to rest, might now move forward and attack the enemy again. Or, if continued fighting appears fruitless, the centuries of *triarii* form a solid line and the whole army retreats in orderly fashion behind the *triarii*'s upraised spears.

In many cases, the charge of the *principes* was enough to win the battle. When it was not enough, these soldiers retreated the same way the *hastati* had and filled the gaps between the *hastati*'s maniples. The Roman commander now had a choice. If he judged that there was still a chance of defeating the enemy, he ordered the *hastati* to advance and charge a second time. Because these men had had some time to rest and gain back their strength, this could be a very effective maneuver. The *principes* might later also have a second go at the enemy, which, more times than not, would eventually give way and flee.

However, if and when the Roman commander decided it was best to quit and fight again another day, he ordered the fresh and very experienced *triarii* to enter the battle. These men formed a solid line, raised their shields, and pointed their spears forward in phalanx fashion, creating a formidable protective barrier. Behind the wall created by the shields and spears of the *triarii*, the rest of the Roman army retreated in an orderly manner.

Rome Versus the Latins, Samnites, and Greeks

During the years of the fourth century B.C., when the Romans were perfecting these highly effective formations and tactics, they were almost always at war with one enemy or another. About 360 B.C., the Gauls intruded into central Italy again, but the Romans drove them away. The Etruscans and Volsci also launched comebacks, all of which were crushed.

Then, in 340 B.C., the Latin League rose against Rome once more. That year, at the Veseris River in Campania (the fertile region south of Latium), a Roman army engaged the Latins. A Roman consul, Titus Manlius held his most experienced veterans in reserve until he was satisfied the enemy troops were exhausted. Then he sent in the fresh veterans, who broke up the opposing formation and inflicted massive casualties. Ancient accounts claim that only a quarter of the Latin army escaped alive. A few months later, Manlius handed the Latins another crushing defeat, from which they never recovered. In 338 B.C. Rome dissolved the Latin League, and one by one the Latin cities came under Roman domination.

These same years also marked the beginning of Rome's three wars against the fierce Samnites, who had long occupied the central and southern Apennines. In 343 B.C. the Samnites attacked Capua (in Campania), and the Capuans appealed to Rome for aid. The war ended two years later with the Romans in complete control of northern Campania.

The Second Samnite War was much longer and bloodier. The conflict began in 326 B.C. when the Samnites occupied Naples (on the coast of Campania). The following year the Romans enjoyed a major victory, killing as many as twenty thousand enemy troops in a single battle. But in 321, at the Caudine Forks (near Capua), the tables were turned. Rome suffered a defeat and the Samnites forced the surviving Romans to walk beneath a yoke, a sign of subjugation and humiliation. Then the Etruscans joined forces with the Samnites, forcing the Romans to fight on two fronts. In the years that followed, however, the Romans rebounded, inflicting major defeats on both enemies.

The Samnites sued for peace in 304 B.C., but just six years later they renewed hostilities, initiating the Third Samnite War. This time, both the Gauls and the Etruscans helped the Samnites, as all three peoples made one last-ditch attempt to stop the increasingly large and effective Roman army. It was a vain effort. The turning point came at Sentinum, in eastern Italy, in 295 B.C. As Polybius sums it up, the Romans "annihilated the greater part of the [enemy] army and scattered the rest in headlong flight, so that each contingent took refuge in its separate territory."[14] Rome then launched a full-scale invasion of the Samnites' mountain heartland, which concluded with the final surrender of the once-mighty Samnites in 290 B.C.

After absorbing most of the former Samnite territories and virtually all of Etruria, Rome controlled most of central and northern Italy. Yet Roman expansion did not end there. The Greek city-states of southern Italy became the next target of Rome's military juggernaut. Most fell without a fight, partly because they had failed to unite into a single, large political and military force, which would have been their only chance

A wall painting dating to the early fourth century B.C. shows Samnite warriors.

against an army as formidable as Rome's. By 265 B.C. the Romans were the undisputed masters of all Italy south of the Po Valley. At the time, a number of foreign observers concluded that Rome would turn next on the empire of Carthage, whose vast fleets of ships controlled the western Mediterranean seaways. And barely a year later, history proved these observers right.

Rome Against Carthage: Round One

T he long, almost relentless conquest of the Italian peninsula by Rome had transformed the Roman army into a formidable machine, one now famous and feared in lands lying well beyond Italy's shores. Polybius, who chronicled the Romans' rise to empire, writes:

> They waged a succession of wars against their neighbors. Through their martial [warlike] valor and consistent success in the [battle]field . . . the Romans . . . subdued the Etruscans and Samnites and defeated the Italian Celts in many battles. . . . The trials of strength they had already experienced . . . had made the Romans veritable champions in the art of war.[15]

These trials had indeed made the Roman military strong, flexible, and resilient. And in 264 B.C. it took the fateful step of venturing outside Italy for the first time. The new target was not merely one more in a series of near neighbors, small-to-moderate-size city-states with relatively limited resources. This time Rome pitted itself against Carthage (centered in Tunisia, in North Africa), a sprawling and powerful empire that, in Polybius's words, "had for generations enjoyed an unchallenged supremacy at sea."[16]

This daring venture marked an important turning point in the history of the Mediterranean world; for now, Rome was no longer just a brash youngster confined to its own backyard. People in all quarters

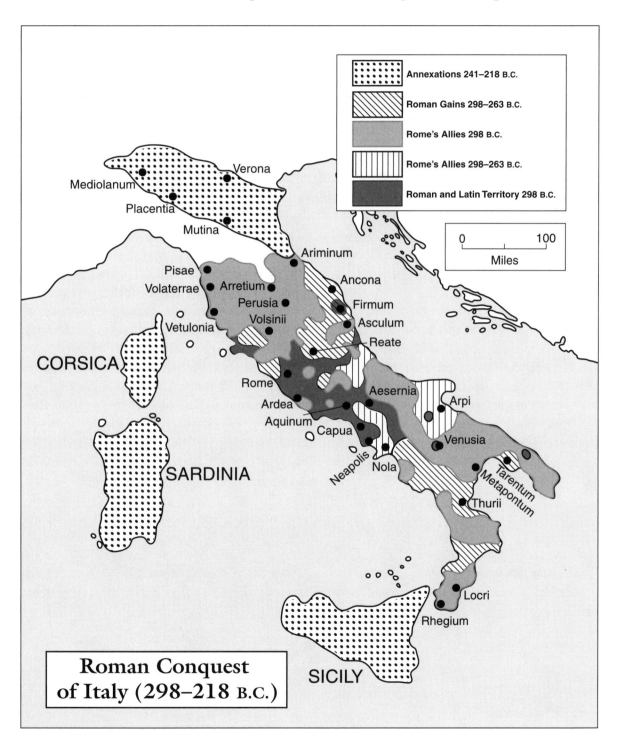

Legend:
- Annexations 241–218 B.C.
- Roman Gains 298–263 B.C.
- Rome's Allies 298 B.C.
- Rome's Allies 298–263 B.C.
- Roman and Latin Territory 298 B.C.

0 — 100
Miles

Mediolanum
Verona
Placentia
Mutina
Ariminum
Pisae
Ancona
Volaterrae
Arretium
Firmum
Perusia
Asculum
Volsinii
Vetulonia
Reate
CORSICA
Rome
Aesernia
Ardea
Arpi
Aquinum
Venusia
Capua
Neapolis
Nola
Tarentum
Metapontum
SARDINIA
Thurii
Locri
Rhegium
SICILY

Roman Conquest of Italy (298–218 B.C.)

of that region now watched the unfolding exploits of the Roman military with growing interest. In time, such interest would become trepidation and eventually a sort of awe, which Polybius describes this way:

> There can surely be nobody so petty or so apathetic in his outlook that he has no desire to discover by what means . . . the Romans succeeded . . . in bringing under their rule almost the whole of the inhabited world, an achievement which is without parallel in human history.[17]

The initial step in this achievement, the first of the three Punic Wars with Carthage, was by far Rome's most difficult test to date. In fact, it was the greatest test any nation had ever faced, one that Rome, despite the strength and toughness of its army, almost did not pass. "It would be difficult to find any contest which was longer in its duration," Polybius states, "more intensively prepared for on both sides, and more unremittingly pursued once begun; or one which involved more battles or more decisive changes of Fortune."[18]

Polybius was right about the war's duration; it turned out to be the longest of all the Greco-Roman conflicts of antiquity. It was also the largest and most devastating war the world had ever witnessed up to that time. It produced at least fifteen major battles, dozens of minor engagements, and hundreds of thousands of casualties. Among other things, the First Punic War proved that war and conquest on the large scale waged by Rome, even when successful, always comes with a high price.

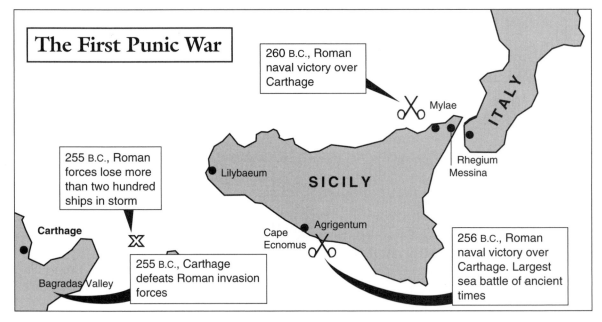

The First Punic War

260 B.C., Roman naval victory over Carthage

Mylae

ITALY

Rhegium
Messina

255 B.C., Roman forces lose more than two hundred ships in storm

Lilybaeum

SICILY

Carthage

Cape Ecnomus

Agrigentum

256 B.C., Roman naval victory over Carthage. Largest sea battle of ancient times

Bagradas Valley

255 B.C., Carthage defeats Roman invasion forces

Trouble in Sicily

The immediate cause of the First Punic War was a dispute surrounding control of the Strait of Messina (or Messana), the narrow waterway separating southeastern Italy from the northern edge of the island of Sicily. Rome needed access to the strait so that fleets of merchant ships could travel easily from Italy's western coasts to its southern and eastern coasts and vice versa. During the late 280s B.C. a band of brigands from Italy's Campania region crossed to Sicily and seized Messina. Calling themselves the Mamertines, or "Sons of Mars," they killed most of the Messinian men, enslaved the women and children, and, in the years that followed, terrorized neighboring towns.

Some of these towns were allies of the powerful Greek city of Syracuse, situated about seventy miles south of Messina. The attacks on his allies eventually forced the hand of Syracuse's king, Heiro. In 265 B.C. he led his army northward and besieged Messina. Things began to grow more complicated when one faction of the Mamertines trapped in the city appealed to Carthage for help. The Carthaginians already controlled much of western Sicily, and they now saw their chance to extend their influence into the island's eastern sphere. Accordingly, a fleet of Carthaginian ships seized control of the strait and, with the help of Heiro and his Syracusans, captured Messina.

This event deeply disturbed the Romans, who saw Carthage's command of the strait as a threat to their security and prosperity. So, not surprisingly, when a second faction of Mamertines, one opposed to the first, asked the Romans for aid, they were only too happy to respond. According to Polybius, the Romans reasoned that

> if the Carthaginians gained control of Sicily, they would prove the most vexatious and dangerous of neighbors, since they would encircle Italy on every side and threaten every part of the country, and this was a prospect which the Romans dreaded. It seemed clear that this would be the fate of Sicily unless help were given to the Mamertines. . . . The Romans foresaw . . . that they should not abandon Messina, and thus allow the Carthaginians to secure a bridgehead for the invasion of Italy.[19]

In Roman eyes, another reason for opposing Carthage in Messina was that the Carthaginians had broken an old agreement between Carthage and Rome. More than a century before, the two nations had signed a treaty assuring that each would stay out of the other's sphere of influence. The agreement had been renewed in 348 B.C. and again in 279. Now, in 264, Rome claimed that Carthage's takeover of Messina had violated the treaty, and the Romans declared war.

The Opposing Forces

As the conflict commenced, both sides felt confident of victory. This may have been because the Romans expected that most

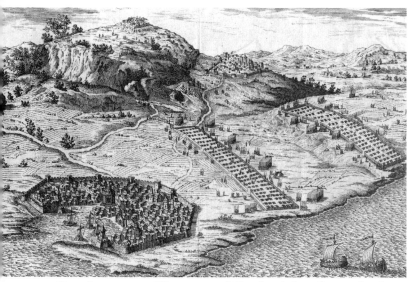

Opposing camps of Romans and Carthaginians face each other in Sicily in the opening stages of the First Punic War.

of the fighting would happen on land whereas the Carthaginians looked forward to a maritime struggle. The fact was that the Romans had the superior land army. In addition to its highly effective manipular tactical system, its soldiers were all citizens of Rome or of the Italian towns in the Roman commonwealth. As such, they could be easily and quickly assembled. But more important, they trained and fought in the same manner, spoke the same language (Latin), and felt they were all defending the same general homeland—Italy.

In contrast, the Carthaginian army was far less unified, organized, or loyal to the state it defended. In fighting other nations, Carthage did not use its own citizens as soldiers (except for generals and some other officers). Instead, it relied partly on subject peoples, especially the inhabitants of

Lybia, which Carthage controlled, and to a larger degree on mercenaries (paid foreign troops). Polybius mentions Ligurians (from the region northwest of Italy), Celts (from what is now southern France), Iberians (Spaniards), Balearic Islanders (from the islands off Spain's eastern coast), Numidians (from Numidia, the kingdom lying west of Carthage in North Africa), and Greeks (from around the Mediterranean world). "How all these troops were armed and organized, it is impossible to say," writes J.F. Lazenby, a noted authority on the Punic Wars.

Presumably the Balearic islanders were slingers, since they were famous for the use of that weapon, and the Numidians already provided cavalry. As the for the rest . . . one may guess that the Greeks . . . were armed as hoplites, i.e. that their main offensive weapon was the . . . thrusting-spear. . . . The Spaniards . . . may have used the formidable cut-and-thrust sword. . . . Spanish skirmishers may have wielded the formidable *phalarica*, from which the Roman *pilum* was allegedly derived. The Celts may similarly have carried their long, slashing swords, and fought naked, or in trousers and cloaks.[20]

Because of these factors, the Carthaginian army took longer to assemble, featured a hodge-podge of soldiers speaking different languages and fighting in diverse styles, and was therefore less reliable than its Roman counterpart.

However, Carthage made up for this deficiency by completely outclassing Rome on the seas. The Carthaginians possessed hundreds of warships, boasted a naval tradition going back centuries, and controlled most of the coasts of the Mediterranean's western portion. These advantages began to show themselves early in the conflict. At the outset, a Roman army commanded by one of the consuls, Appius Claudius, marched to Rhegium and then used fishing boats to cross the strait. The Romans rather handily defeated the Carthaginians and Syracusans in a land battle and captured Messina. But when Rome tried to extend its conquest to other sectors of Sicily, it learned the hard

way how effective sea power could be. Carthaginian warships blockaded Sicilian ports, severing Roman supply lines. As the months rolled by, Roman troops grew hungry and short of proper equipment, their morale suffered, and their offensive campaign eventually ground to a halt.

A Fleet Built with Amazing Speed

Eventually, Roman leaders saw that there was only one way to drive the enemy out of Sicily and win the war: Rome must build its own fleets of warships. For a nation with no warships at all, no naval tradition, and no trained naval officers, to launch so huge and bold an initiative was surprising and impressive enough. What made it truly amazing was the speed at which the task was accomplished. The first

This nineteenth-century engraving reconstructs the city of Carthage at the height of its power. Its great circular harbor and naval station are visible in the distance.

fleet, consisting of 120 ships, was completed in only sixty days. Polybius says that one hundred of these were quinqueremes and the other twenty, triremes. (A trireme featured three banks of oars with one man to an oar; a quinquereme, which was larger, most likely had three banks of oars, with two men to an oar in the upper two banks and one to an oar in the lower bank.) "They faced great difficulties," Polybius writes, "because their shipwrights were completely inexperienced in the building of quinqueremes, since these vessels had never before been employed in Italy." Fortunately for the Romans, though, they got their hands on a Carthaginian quinquereme that had run aground. "It was this ship which they proceeded to use as a model, and they built their whole fleet according to its specifications."[21]

Polybius also tells how the Roman army trained its soldiers to operate the warships:

Those who had been given the task of shipbuilding occupied themselves with the construction work, while others collected the crews and began to teach them to row on shore. . . . They placed the men along the rowers' benches on dry land, seating them in the same order as if they were on those of an actual vessel, and . . . they trained them to swing back their bodies in unison bringing their hands up in front of them, then to move forwards again thrusting their hands in front of them, and to begin and end these movements at the command of the *keleustes* [a man who used a mallet to pound out a rhythm for the rowers to follow]. When the crews had learned this drill, the ships

These warships, which used both sails and oars, were typical of those built by the Carthaginians and Romans during the first of their three conflicts.

were launched as soon as they were finished . . . [and] spent a short time on rowing practice actually at sea.[22]

The Romans also prepared for the coming fight by creating a secret weapon. They knew that the chief offensive naval tactic was for one ship to ram another, opening a hole in the enemy vessel's hull and thereby causing it to sink. A more difficult but not uncommon maneuver was to come up alongside the enemy ship and board it. Roman military officers reasoned that Carthage's superior naval experience would give its ships the advantage in ramming.

On the other hand, if Roman legionaries could board an enemy ship and fight as they did on land, *they* would have the advantage. The trick was to devise an effective way to deliver the troops to the decks of the enemy vessels. The result was the *corvus*, or "raven," a long wooden gangway with a spike attached to its end. The device stood upright on the deck of a Roman ship until the vessel pulled up alongside an enemy ship, at which time sailors dropped the device onto the enemy's deck. The spike pierced the deck, holding the gangway in place, and Roman soldiers charged across and attacked the enemy vessel's crew.

Rome on the Offensive

The rapid construction of warships, training of the crews, and invention of the *corvus* marked the start of an important new phase in the evolution of Rome's military. These moves gave it at least an even chance of beating one of the world's leading naval powers. "It is this fact which illustrates better than any other the extraordinary spirit and audacity of the Romans' decision," Polybius points out.

> It was not a question of having adequate resources for the enterprise, for they had in fact none whatsoever, nor had they ever given a thought to the sea before this. But once they had conceived the idea, they embarked on it so boldly, that without waiting to gain any experience in naval warfare they immediately engaged the Carthaginians.[23]

This initial engagement between the opposing fleets took place in the summer of 260 B.C. near Mylae, on Sicily's northeastern coast. The Roman commander, Gaius Duilius, took a daring risk by committing his entire fleet of 120 ships in a headlong attack. According to Polybius, the Carthaginians had 130 ships and

> their spirits were high, for at this stage they felt nothing but contempt for the inexperience of the Romans. . . . As they neared the enemy and saw the "ravens" hoisted aloft in the bows of several ships, the Carthaginians at first did not know what to make of these devices. . . . However, as they still felt an utter contempt for their opponents, the leading ships attacked without hesitation. Then, as they came into collision, the Carthaginians found that their vessels

A Carthaginian ship is held fast and boarded by Roman troops during the first large sea battle of the war.

they had a fleet large enough to invade Africa and take Carthage.

In preparation for that invasion, in 256 B.C. a huge Roman force consisting of 330 ships and 140,000 men sailed to Cape Ecnomus in southern Sicily. The Carthaginians tried to counter this move by bringing up an even larger force, which Polybius estimates at 350 ships and 150,000 men. These figures may be exaggerated, as Polybius, who lived a century later, got his information second- and third-hand. Modern experts estimate that each side had between two hundred and three hundred vessels. The battle that followed was the largest naval encounter fought anywhere in the world in ancient times. The Romans won, destroying about thirty enemy ships and capturing sixty others along with their crews.

Roman Setbacks

Having pushed the main Carthaginian fleet aside, the Romans had cleared the way for their attack on the enemy's homeland. In the summer of 256 B.C. the consul Marcus Atilius Regulus landed in North Africa with about fifteen thousand infantry and five hundred cavalry and immediately began plundering the countryside. Soon he besieged and captured the town of Adys (southeast of Carthage) and easily defeated a small army of Carthaginian mercenaries sent to stop him. To raise more troops would take time, so Carthage, which had been too confident

were invariably held fast by the "ravens," and the Roman troops swarmed aboard them . . . and fought them hand-to-hand on deck. Some of the Carthaginians were cut down and others were thrown into confusion . . . and gave themselves up, for the fighting seemed to have been transformed into a battle on dry land. . . . The Carthaginians turned and fled, for they were completely unnerved by these new tactics, and in all they lost fifty ships.[24]

In Carthage, leaders and ordinary citizens alike were shocked to hear that one of their fleets had been defeated by the land-lubbing Romans. Though embarrassed and dismayed, the Carthaginians rose to the challenge. They redeployed their remaining ships and built many more. Meanwhile, during the next three years the Romans continued to turn out more warships of their own until they were confident that in the power of its navy and unprepared for an enemy land attack, was now very vulnerable.

However, Regulus was also guilty of overconfidence. First, his forces were too small to conquer and hold the large metropolis of Carthage and the many populous cities surrounding it. Also, he failed to strike immediately at the capital while the enemy was still unprepared. Instead, the Romans spent the winter ravaging villages and farms in the countryside, and that gave the Carthaginians time to raise a new army. In the spring of 255 B.C. a hired Greek general named Xanthippus put together a force composed of Greeks and other mercenaries and some native Carthaginians. This army, which numbered some twelve thousand infantry, four thousand cavalry, and one hundred battle elephants, attacked the Romans in the Bagradas Valley, southeast of Carthage. Regulus arrayed his troops in the usual manipular fashion, but he failed to anticipate the strength of the enemy's elephants and horsemen. The elephants trampled through the front maniples, breaking them up, while the Carthaginian cavalry encircled the Roman wings, outflanking and surrounding most of the Roman army. All

Roman warships sink several Carthaginian vessels and capture many more in the huge naval battle of Cape Ecnomus. The Romans then launched an invasion of North Africa.

but two thousand of Regulus's troops were killed. By contrast, Xanthippus lost only eight hundred men.

Horrified by this unexpected defeat, Roman leaders mustered most of their remaining ships—some 350 according to Polybius—and launched a rescue mission. This enormous fleet did manage to pick up most of Regulus's surviving men. But on the way back to Sicily, Polybius writes, the ships

ran into a fearful storm and suffered a disaster on a scale that almost beggars description. . . . Only eighty [of their ships] survived. The rest either foundered or were hurled by the waves against the rocks and headlands, where they broke up, leaving the shore heaped with corpses and wreckage.[25]

This setback proved only the first of many for the Romans in the years that followed. They lost fleet after fleet in violent storms. And because they constantly had to construct new ships and train new crews, the conflict dragged

The Price for Abandoning the *Corvus*

Though an extremely effective aid to the Roman military, the corvus *was heavy and cumbersome and made Roman ships unbalanced and prone to capsizing, especially in rough seas. So, after losing hundreds of warships in a series of storms, Rome eliminated all* corvi *from its navy during the late 250s B.C. This move had negative consequences in the short run, as explained here by military historian Simon Anglim in his book* Fighting Techniques of the Ancient World.

Without the *corvus*, the poorer quality of the Romans' ships and training became obvious at the battle of Drepanum in 249 B.C., Rome's only serious sea defeat. The Roman consul Publius Claudius Pulcher, with about 123 ships under his command, mounted a surprise attack on the main Carthaginian naval base at Drepanum. . . . The Carthaginians saw the Roman fleet coming and put to sea to confront the enemy. . . . Superior training then showed. . . . The Roman ships, trying to form into battle-line, were in great confusion, many fouling each other. A ramming battle then developed. The Roman ships did not have the room or the skill to maneuver and avoid the Carthaginian rams, and no longer had the *corvi* to engage in their typical boarding attack. Only 30 of the Roman ships, including Claudius Pulcher's flagship, managed to escape.

on and on. The Romans also suffered a serious naval defeat near Drepanum, on Sicily's western coast, in 249 B.C., losing ninety-three ships. What is more, two years later a brilliant military leader named Hamilcar Barca took charge of Carthage's war effort in Sicily. Barca led frequent successful raids against Roman positions on the coasts of Sicily and Italy, causing much mayhem.

A Do-or-Die Spirit

By 241 B.C. Roman manpower, resources, and money were exhausted, and it looked as though Carthage would win the war. However, the Romans still possessed one last resource—a spirit of resolve and a refusal to admit defeat, even in the face of overwhelming odds, that have seldom been matched in human history. With the state treasury empty, citizens from all walks of life opened their pockets to finance one last all-or-nothing fleet. Commanded by the consul Gaius Lutatius Catulus, this force daringly attacked the main Carthaginian fleet near the Aegates Islands off Sicily's western coast. Catulus won an overwhelming victory, sinking fifty enemy ships and capturing another seventy along with their crews.

With their main fleet virtually eliminated, Carthage could no longer supply its bases in Sicily, nor could it defend itself against the Roman invasion of North Africa that was sure to follow. Thus, the Carthaginians acknowledged defeat and had to cede Sicily to Rome. They also had

A reconstruction of Roman Legionaries from the period of the Second Punic War.

to pay the Romans a yearly war reparation of thirty-two hundred talents, an enormous sum at the time. At the eleventh hour, the Romans had gambled everything on their military prowess and do-or-die spirit and won an important foothold in the larger Mediterranean world. Soon, they would exploit that advantage to its fullest in a new and still larger cycle of expansion.

Rome Against Carthage: Round Two

As an instrument of power, the Roman military had first given Rome control of all Italy except the Po Valley. Then the army won the large, fertile island of Sicily (except for Syracuse and a few other Greek cities on the island, which for the moment remained independent). "This annexation of Sicily was a fateful step," Michael Grant points out,

for it brought the Romans outside Italy, of which the island was not in ancient times a part, and gave them their first overseas province. An entirely new and lasting stage in Roman history had begun an epoch [era] of imperialism outside the mother country.[26]

At first, this new tendency toward territorial and political expansion was not deliberately planned by the Roman government. As historian Chester G. Starr puts it:

Many Roman leaders, indeed, spoke against foreign entanglements and commitments in terms we might well call "isolationist." Yet internal expansive forces were strong and were further intensified by the unstable political conditions which existed elsewhere in the Mediterranean.[27]

In other words, the Romans steadily took advantage of enticing opportunities that arose in their neighborhood as a result of troubles happening elsewhere.

Almost immediately after the end of the First Punic War, for example, Carthage experienced a severe internal crisis. A large group of its mercenaries who had not been paid rebelled, and it took Hamilcar Barca and a small army of loyal troops many months of horrendously bloody fighting to quell the uprising. Rome did not interfere. But in 238 B.C. other former Carthaginian mercenaries on the large island of Sardinia (lying off Italy's western coast), which Carthage controlled, appealed to Rome for help. This time, Rome seized the opportunity by annexing the island, along with Corsica (the island just north of Sardinia). Carthage naturally protested, but the Romans threatened war. At the time, Carthage was in no shape to wage another large-scale conflict, so it was forced to sit back and allow part of its empire to be stripped away. The Roman army had become so formidable that the mere threat of its use was a potent tool in Rome's foreign policy.

That army was far from idle, however. Rome sent it into Illyria (the region east of the Adriatic Sea) in 229 B.C. to wipe out pirate strongholds, and while there, the soldiers set up permanent military bases. Four years later, responding to intermittent raids into Roman territory by Gauls from the Po Valley, a Roman army marched into the valley and in the span of five years conquered it. Nations and empires across the Mediterranean world now began to

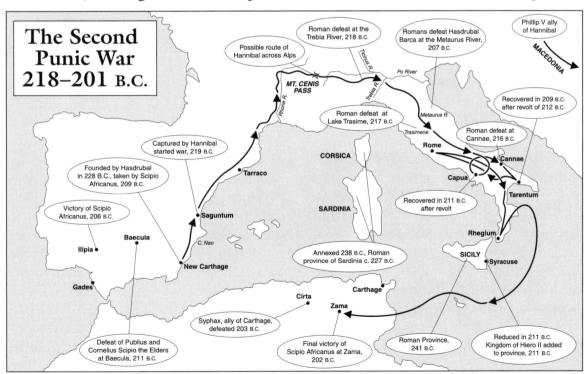

The Second Punic War 218–201 B.C.

- Possible route of Hannibal across Alps
- Roman defeat at the Trebia River, 218 B.C.
- Romans defeat Hasdrubal Barca at the Metaurus River, 207 B.C.
- Phillip V ally of Hannibal
- MACEDONIA
- MT. CENIS PASS
- Ticinus R.
- Po River
- Trebia R.
- Rhone R.
- Roman defeat at Lake Trasime, 217 B.C.
- Metaurus R.
- Recovered in 209 B.C. after revolt of 212 B.C.
- Trasimene
- Roman defeat at Cannae, 216 B.C.
- CORSICA
- Rome
- Cannae
- Captured by Hannibal started war, 219 B.C.
- Founded by Hasdrubal in 228 B.C., taken by Scipio Africanus, 209 B.C.
- Tarraco
- Capua
- Tarentum
- Victory of Scipio Africanus, 206 B.C.
- Saguntum
- SARDINIA
- Recovered in 211 B.C. after revolt
- Baecula
- C. Nao
- Rhegium
- Ilipia
- New Carthage
- Annexed 238 B.C., Roman province of Sardinia c. 227 B.C.
- SICILY
- Syracuse
- Gades
- Cirta
- Carthage
- Zama
- Syphax, ally of Carthage, defeated 203 B.C.
- Defeat of Publius and Cornelius Scipio the Elders at Baecula, 211 B.C.
- Final victory of Scipio Africanus at Zama, 202 B.C.
- Roman Province, 241 B.C.
- Reduced in 211 B.C. Kingdom of Hiero II added to province, 211 B.C.

watch Rome's continuing expansion with a wary eye.

The Carthaginians in Spain

Not least among these observers were the Carthaginians, who had suffered more than anyone else at Roman hands. Hamilcar Barca was particularly bitter over Rome's victory in the first Punic conflict, the annexation of Sicily, and what he saw as the outright theft of Sardinia and Corsica. Hamilcar swore that he would get revenge on Rome sooner or later. Out of sheer necessity, he came to realize, it would have to be later, as first he would have to restore Carthage to its former strength and prestige.

To accomplish this task, Hamilcar decided to build a new power base in Spain, where Carthage already had considerable influence. In 237 B.C. he landed his small army at Gades, in southwestern Spain, and in only a few years managed to conquer most of the southern half of the Iberian Peninsula. Along the way, Hamilcar wisely enlisted Spanish natives into his growing army. He paid them well from the assets he gained from Spain's rich silver mines and also sent large amounts of money back to Carthage, helping to revitalize it.

In addition, Hamilcar tried to ensure that his plans to strike back at Rome would go forward even if he died. He did this by grooming his son, Hannibal Barca, to succeed him. At his father's urgings, Hannibal swore on an altar eternal hatred for the Romans. This would eventually have grave consequences for Rome, for Hannibal would soon prove himself to be one of the greatest military leaders of all times. About the grown Hannibal, Livy later wrote:

> Under his leadership, the men invariably showed to the best advantage both dash and confidence. Reckless in courting danger, he showed superb tactical ability once it was upon him. Indefatigable [untiring] both physically and mentally, he could endure with equal ease excessive heat or excessive cold. . . . Often he was seen lying in his cloak on the bare ground amongst the common soldiers. . . . Mounted or unmounted, he was unequalled as a fighting man, always the first to attack, [and] the last to leave the field.[28]

Hamilcar did not live to see these qualities in his son fully realized. In 229 B.C. the elder Barca drowned. However, Hannibal, then about eighteen, was seen as too young to take command of Carthage's forces in Spain, and this duty fell to Hamilcar's son-in-law, Hasdrubal. Hasdrubal continued the conquest of the peninsula. This worried the Romans, who correctly suspected that Carthage had designs on southern Europe. So during the mid-220s B.C., hoping to create a barrier to further Carthaginian expansion in the area, Rome made an alliance with Saguntum, a city on Spain's eastern coast.

This move proved fruitless. In 221 B.C. Hasdrubal was assassinated by a discontented Spanish native, and Hannibal finally took charge of Carthaginian Spain. The following year, Hannibal attacked and besieged Saguntum and rudely rebuffed a delegation from Rome that demanded that he desist and withdraw. In 219 the city fell, and a few months later, early in 218, the Romans declared war. The greatest test yet, for both Rome's army and the determination and courage of the Roman people, had begun.

The Element of Surprise

As they had been at the start of the first war with Carthage, the Romans were confident of victory. Roman leaders decided on a twofold strategy designed to cripple both of Carthage's main power bases and bring the conflict to a swift conclusion. One Roman army would cross to North Africa and attack Carthage; meanwhile, another large Roman force would sail from Italy to southern Gaul and march southward to assault Hannibal's Spanish stronghold.

The second of these operations was progressing well when one of Rome's consuls, Publius Cornelius Scipio, landed an army near the mouth of the Rhone River (in southern Gaul) in April 218 B.C. Scipio was shocked to learn that Hannibal and his own army had recently passed within only fifty miles of the Roman position. The Romans hurried in pursuit. But they were unable to catch up with Hannibal, who was heading northeast, straight for the Alps. It had not occurred to the Romans that the enemy would make such a move because they viewed the Alps as a barrier no army could ever hope to cross intact.

This element of surprise, of course, was exactly what the brilliant and wily Hannibal had been counting on. In September 218 B.C., he led about forty thousand men, hundreds of horses, and thirty-seven elephants across the Alps in an endeavor that was as dangerous as it was audacious. On reaching the highest point in the journey, Livy wrote,

Hannibal ferries his men and elephants across the Rhone River, in southern Gaul, on his way to crossing the Alps.

45

there was a two-days' halt on the summit, to rest the men after the exhausting climb. . . . The troops had indeed endured hardships enough, but there was worse to come. . . . As in most parts of the Alps, the descent on the Italian side . . . is correspondingly steeper, [so] the going was much more difficult than it had been during the ascent. The track was almost everywhere precipitous [steep], narrow, and slippery; it was impossible for a man to keep his feet; the least stumble meant a fall, and a fall a slide, so that there was indescribable confusion, men and beast stumbling and slipping on top of each other.[29]

As Hannibal invaded northern Italy, the Romans chose Quintus Fabius Maximus (on the horse) as dictator.

Despite incredible hardships and heavy losses, including more than a third of his men and most of the elephants, Hannibal made it to northern Italy by October. His forces now numbered some twenty thousand infantry and six thousand cavalry. Scipio, who had sent his own army on to Spain and hurried back to Italy, met with the other consul, Tiberius Sempronius Longus, to map out a strategy to halt the enemy advance.

But their efforts were in vain. As Hannibal approached the Ticinus River (a tributary of the Po), Scipio went out ahead of his own army with a force of horsemen to scout the situation. This unit suddenly encountered Hannibal, who was leading his own Numidian horseman in a similar scouting mission. In the ensuing battle, according to Livy, the Numidians "executed an encircling movement and appeared in the Roman rear. It was a severe blow to the Roman morale, and the situation was made worse by the fact that Scipio was wounded."[30]

Though this Roman defeat had been relatively small, the next two were much larger and more crippling. Leading fresh troops, Longus met Hannibal at the nearby Trebia River, where the Carthaginian general set a clever trap. Hannibal used a force of horsemen to lure the Romans out of their

Hannibal Urges His Troops On

In this excerpt from Livy's great history of Rome (excerpted in Livy: The War with Hannibal*), as Hannibal and his troops face the rugged, dangerous passage through the Alps, he gives them a pep talk, telling them that their goal—Italy—is closer at hand than they think.*

Now, when you can see that much of the greater part of the distance is already behind you . . . when finally you have the Alps in sight, and know that the other side of them is Italian soil . . . at the very gateway of the enemy's country, you come to a halt, exhausted! What do you think the Alps *are*? Are they anything worse than high mountains? Say, if you will, that they are higher than the Pyrenees [situated between Spain and France], but what of it? No part of earth reaches the sky. . . . Moreover, the Alps are not desert. Men live there; they till the ground; there are animals there, living creatures. If a small party can cross them, surely armies can? . . . [It is] Rome, the mightiest city of the world, [which] you aim to conquer. How can you feel that anything, however hard, however dangerous, can make you hesitate?

camp, after which Longus ordered his men to wade through the river's icy waters to reach the enemy on the far side. After the wet, numb, and exhausted Romans engaged the enemy, Hannibal sprang the trap. His brother, Mago Barca, led a second force of Carthaginians from a concealed position and fell on the Roman army's rear. Of the estimated forty thousand Roman troops involved in the struggle, only about ten thousand escaped. Following this disaster, Hannibal delivered the Romans still another devastating defeat at Lake Trasimene, situated only seventy miles north of Rome. In this encounter, about fifteen thousand Roman soldiers died and a similar number were taken prisoner.

The Man Who Refused to Fight

Hannibal's losses in these battles had been small. And he was now in a strategic position to strike at the capital city of his hated enemy. The Romans reacted by appointing a dictator (who would serve for only six months). He was a republican official chosen in an emergency and given sweeping powers to save the country from impending disaster. The man selected for the job was Quintus Fabius Maximus, a nobleman with a reputation for honesty and sound judgment. Fabius hastily destroyed the bridges leading to Rome and burned all the crops in the area so that Hannibal would have difficulty feeding his own troops during a siege.

Hannibal surprised the Romans again, however, by not pressing a siege of their capital. Instead, he bypassed Rome and marched into south-central Italy, where he hoped to gain the support of some of the hill peoples the Romans had conquered during the preceding century. He judged, probably correctly, that without these allies, whose men made up close to half of the Roman army, Rome would be fatally weakened.

In the meantime, Fabius saw that the Roman military was already badly weakened by its recent losses to Hannibal. In an effort to avoid losing any more soldiers, the dictator instituted a new, more prudent policy for dealing with the invaders. He "was determined not to fight a pitched battle," Plutarch wrote in his biography of Fabius,

and since he had time . . . on his side, his plan was to exhaust his opponent's strength . . . by means of delaying tactics, and gradually to wear down his small army and meager resources. With this object in view, he always camped in mountainous country, where he was out of the reach of the enemy's cavalry, and at the same time hung menacingly over the Carthaginian camp. If the enemy stayed still, he did the same. If they moved, he would make a detour, descend a little distance from the heights, and show himself just far enough away to prevent himself from being forced into action against his will,

but near enough to create the suspicion . . . that he might be about to attack.[31]

These tactics were effective, but they grew increasingly unpopular with the Roman people. Hannibal's soldiers often burned farms and villages in plain sight of Roman troops, who, by order of the dictator, were not allowed to get involved. Many Romans came to the mistaken belief that Fabius was afraid to fight. So when Fabius dutifully laid down his six-month appointment at the end of 217 B.C., the Roman people elected new consuls who promised to reverse his policy of refusing to engage Hannibal.

Rome's Worst Defeat

Eager to prove themselves, these consuls, Gaius Terentius Varro and Lucius Aemilius Paullus, gathered a huge army. Their force, which may have numbered seventy thousand or more, then marched on Hannibal, who was camped at Cannae in southeastern Italy. With forty-five thousand troops at most (including several thousand Gauls who had joined him in Po Valley), the Carthaginian leader was clearly outnumbered. Yet when the two armies met on August 2, 216 B.C., he engineered a truly stunning victory. Hannibal showed that a Roman manipular army, though extremely flexible and efficient, was only as good as its commanders and could be outmaneuvered by a more clever general.

As the two armies neared each other, for instance, Hannibal saw that Varro and Paullus had arrayed their troops in standard manipular fashion, with the infantry in the center and small detachments of cavalry on the wings. (The main task of the cavalry was to guard the flanks of the Roman infantry and keep enemy horsemen from riding around and behind the infantry.) Hannibal knew that the Roman infantry would charge forward and try to overwhelm his own center. So he set a trap for it. Instead of placing his strongest infantry, the Africans, in the center, he held these troops in reserve on the flanks and put his less formidable Spanish and Celtic infantry in the center.

The battle began as most formal pitched battles did in those days—with light-armed skirmishers from each side running forward and hurling javelins and other projectiles. Then, executing the usual manipular tactic, the Roman *hastati* closed ranks and charged the Carthaginian center. They easily pushed the enemy back. And the rest of the Romans, still arrayed in their maniples, moved forward behind them, ready to enter the fight if needed. At this point, the Roman legionaries did not realize that the Carthaginian horsemen had lured away the Roman cavalry units, bested them, and begun to chase them off the field. That left the maniples of Roman infantry with no one to guard their flanks.

Most of the necessary elements were now in place for Hannibal to close the trap. As he watched, the front ranks of Roman legionaries, as he had anticipated, drove the Carthaginian center back so far that it passed between his elite troops, the Africans, who were still stationed on the flanks. These fresh troops now turned inward and assaulted the sides of the Roman maniples, which began to lose their cohesion. At the same time, the Carthaginian cavalry, which by now had driven away the Roman cavalry, attacked the rear of the Roman army. Encircled by the enemy, the Roman ranks fell into chaos, and the Carthaginians butchered as many as they could. "After that," Livy writes, "there was nothing but men flying for their lives. . . . The total number of casualties is said to have been 45,500 infantrymen and 2,700 cavalrymen killed."[32] Among these dead were the consul Paullus and some eighty senators; in contrast, Hannibal lost only six thousand men. Without doubt, the defeat at Cannae was the worst single military defeat in Rome's long history.

The Romans Rebound

After the Roman catastrophe at Cannae, Hannibal seemed on the brink of winning a total victory in the war. Yet three major factors worked against him and eventually saved Rome. First, as he had following his victories at the Trebia River and Lake Trasimene, Hannibal failed to march on Rome after his win at Cannae. He probably reasoned that he was ill prepared to prosecute so great a siege; after all, he had no ships, no siege equipment, and no permanent supply bases near Rome. So Hannibal chose to go on pillaging the Italian countryside and urging Rome's allies to defect to his cause. The large-scale defections he needed never occurred, however.

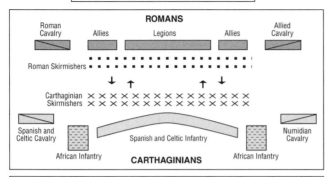

Battle of Cannae

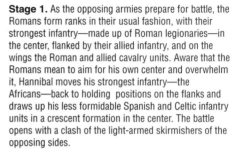

Stage 1. As the opposing armies prepare for battle, the Romans form ranks in their usual fashion, with their strongest infantry—made up of Roman legionaries—in the center, flanked by their allied infantry, and on the wings the Roman and allied cavalry units. Aware that the Romans mean to aim for his own center and overwhelm it, Hannibal moves his strongest infantry—the Africans—back to holding positions on the flanks and draws up his less formidable Spanish and Celtic infantry units in a crescent formation in the center. The battle opens with a clash of the light-armed skirmishers of the opposing sides.

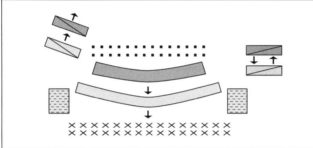

Stage 2. After the initial, indecisive exchange between the skirmishers, per the usual procedure they retreat to the rear and the opposing infantry units advance on each other. The Roman legions and allied units push the weaker Carthaginian center backward, just as Hannibal had anticipated they would, while he shrewdly continues to hold his Africans in reserve. Meanwhile, the cavalry units on the right clash, while on the left the Roman cavalry breaks and flees from the numerically superior Spanish and Celtic cavalry.

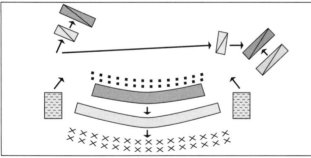

Stage 3. As the Roman infantrymen continue to press forward, believing they are winning the battle, Hannibal's brilliant trap begins to spring on them. With the added support of his skirmishers in the rear, his center holds. At the same time, his Africans turn toward the center and begin to envelop the Roman flanks. Meanwhile, as a small contingent of his Spanish and Celtic cavalry pursues the Roman horsemen off the field, the rest swing behind the Roman army and attack the Roman allied cavalry from the rear.

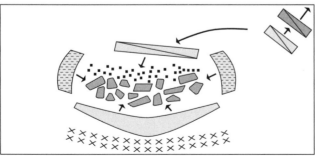

Stage 4. Assaulted front and back by the enemy, the Roman allied cavalry breaks and flees, pursued by Hannibal's Numidians. His Spanish and Celtic cavalry then wheels around and attacks the Roman center from behind. Now nearly surrounded, the normally disciplined Roman ranks fall apart and a massive slaughter ensues. Some 50,000 Romans are killed, the largest single battlefield loss in Rome's history, while Hannibal, whose victory is complete, loses only 6,000 to 7,000 men.

Second, Italy was a large, fertile country blessed with many natural resources. The Romans still controlled most of the peninsula and could exploit its ports, rivers, and farmland to their advantage. With such abundant supplies at their disposal, they could raise and train new armies that, sooner or later, could wear down Hannibal's forces.

The third factor working in Rome's favor was its renowned spirit of determination. Despite their recent series of terrible defeats, Livy says, the Romans refused to utter a word about peace or surrender:

> So great, in this grim time, was the nation's heart, that the consul [Varro, who had survived Cannae], fresh from a defeat of which he had himself been the principal cause, was met on his return to Rome by people of all conditions to participate in the thanks publicly bestowed on him for not having "despaired of the commonwealth." A Carthaginian general in such circumstances would have been [severely] punished.[33]

For these reasons, the Romans steadily rebounded during the years following Cannae, which was fortunate for them considering that they had to fight the widening war on many fronts. In Italy, of course, the main threat was still Hannibal.

To deal with him, the Romans fell back on Fabius's proven policy of delay, harassment, and containment. Over time, Fabius and another widely respected general, Marcus Claudius Marcellus, worked out an effective twofold strategy. While Fabius relentlessly wore down the invaders, at intervals Marcellus suddenly attacked them when and where they least expected it. This approach more or less neutralized Hannibal, who grew increasingly frustrated.

Publius Cornelius Scipio the Younger, whose campaigns in North Africa earned him the nickname "Africanus."

Meanwhile, the Romans had to contend with the Greek kingdom of Macedonia (encompassing most of mainland Greece). In 215 B.C. Hannibal made a pact with its king, Philip V, who promised to attack southern Italy and help the Carthaginians conquer the peninsula. The following year, however, the Romans beat Philip to the punch; they crossed to Illyria, where he was assembling his invasion force, drove him away, and burned his ships.

Another important front was in Spain, site of the Barcas' power base. After fighting Hannibal at the Ticinus River in 218 B.C., Scipio journeyed to Spain, where he and his brother, Gnaeus, led Roman forces against Hannibal's own brother, Hasdrubal Barca. At first, the Romans were successful. They captured many enemy strongholds, including Saguntum, whose capture by Hannibal had ignited the conflict. But then Carthage sent massive reinforcements to Spain and the Scipio brothers were defeated and killed in battle. Taking their place was Publius Cornelius Scipio the Younger, a brilliant military tactician. He reversed the situation, defeated Hasdrubal, and by 206 B.C. captured all of Carthaginian Spain.

The War's Shattering Conclusion

Two years later Scipio served his country again by opening still another front, this one the most pivotal in the conflict. The revitalized and once more powerful Roman military finally carried the war to the enemy's homeland. Scipio established an initial base of operations in Sicily and from there used four hundred troop transports and forty warships to ferry an invasion force of thirty thousand troops to the North African coast near Utica, only twenty-five miles west of Carthage. The Romans besieged and captured Utica, then pillaged the Carthaginian countryside. Scipio also allied himself with a Numidian prince, Masinissa, who both hated Carthage and commanded a formidable cavalry force.

With his country under direct attack, Hannibal felt he had no choice but to leave Italy and return to Africa. In the spring of 202 B.C. he and Scipio faced each other on the plain of Zama, about seventy-five miles southwest of Carthage. The Carthaginian forces numbered about forty thousand men and eighty elephants while the Romans and Masinissa's Numidians totaled perhaps thirty-six thousand. The Roman infantry was arrayed in manipular fashion, in three distinct lines, and Hannibal also arranged his men in three lines.

The battle opened with a charge by the Carthaginian elephants, but their effectiveness was blunted when Roman trumpeters created a din that frightened and dispersed the beasts. Next, the Roman and Numidian cavalry, stationed on Scipio's wings, attacked Hannibal's horsemen and chased them away, leaving his infantry exposed. Scipio's first line of infantry then charged and easily pushed back Hannibal's own first line. Hannibal's second line was more of a match for the legionaries. But

Battle of Zama 202 B.C.

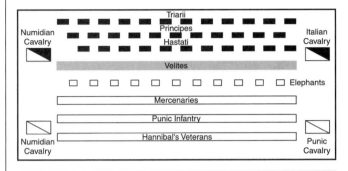

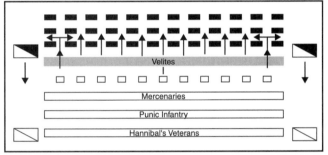

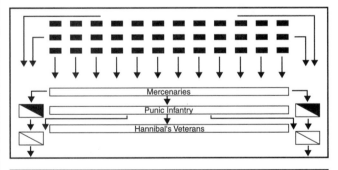

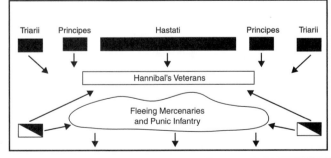

Stage 1: Scipio draws up his army in three main lines in *quincunx* formation with the *triarii* in reserve, his *velites* in front, the Italian cavalry on his left flank, and Masinissa's Numidian cavalry on his right flank. Hannibal deploys his eighty elephants in front of the first line of mercenaries. Behind them in a second line he places his Punic infantry and behind them in the third line stand his veterans. He positions his Numidian and Punic cavalry on his left and right flanks respectively. The battle begins when Hannibal orders his elephants to charge the Roman lines.

Stage 2: As the elephants charge, Scipio has his *principe* line shift laterally so as to form alleys between the Roman maniples. The *velites* fall back through the gaps and fill in the spaces between the maniples. And as the elephants charge by, they are met with missile-fire from three sides, trumpets blare, and legionaries attempt to hamstring them. This causes the elephants to panic and bolt back into the Carthaginian lines. Some pass harmlessly through the Roman formation, others die under a hail of missile-fire.

Stage 3: On the flanks, the Roman cavalry charges into the Carthaginian cavalry and drives them away, pursuing them off the battlefield. Scipio orders is infantry to charge Hannibal's mercenaries, forcing them back on the line of Punic infantry. They close ranks and force the mercenaries to retreat to the sides, causing confusion. The Romans force the second line to fall back and around Hannibal's veterans. Scipio then widens his front by moving the *principes* and *triarii* to the flanks, extending his line.

Stage 4: Scipio's legionaries charge Hannibal's veterans as the Numidian and Roman cavalry return to the field and attack Hannibal's line in the rear. The last of Hannibal's line collapses, and the Carthaginian army is slaughtered in the ensuing pursuit.

the Romans eventually defeated them and advanced on Hannibal and his veterans in the third line. As this infantry battle raged on, Masinissa and his horsemen, having eliminated Hannibal's cavalry, suddenly returned and attacked the Carthaginians from behind. This proved Hannibal's undoing. Polybius reports:

> The greater number of his men were cut down in their ranks, while of those who took to flight only a few escaped, since the cavalry were close upon their heels. . . . The Romans lost over 1,500 men, but of the Carthaginians more than 20,000 were killed and almost as many taken prisoner.[34]

Hannibal's first and only defeat brought the Second Punic War, the greatest conflict the world had yet seen, to a shattering conclusion. Roman armies had won impressive victories all over the central and western Mediterranean, gaining

Hannibal's elephants charge the Roman lines in the opening phase of the battle of Zama. Using their javelins, the Romans slew many of the huge beasts.

Carthage Accepts the Peace Treaty

Here, from his Histories, *Polybius lists some of the terms of the treaty that ended the Second Punic War and Hannibal's reaction to them.*

The Carthaginians were to pay reparations to the Romans for all acts of injustice committed during the truce; prisoners of war and deserters who had fallen into their hands at any time were to be handed over; all their elephants and all ships of war with the exception of ten triremes were to be surrendered; they were not to make war on any people outside Africa at all, and on none in Africa without consent from Rome. . . . "It seems to me amazing," [Hannibal told the Carthaginian senators] . . . that anyone who is a citizen of Carthage . . . should not thank his stars that now that we are at their mercy, we have obtained such lenient terms. If you had been asked only a few days ago . . . what you expected your country would suffer in the event of a Roman victory . . . you would not even have been able to express your fears. So now I beg you not even to debate the question, but to declare your acceptance of the proposals unanimously." . . . All the senators considered that this advice was well-conceived . . . [and] sent out envoys with instructions to accept the terms.

Rome huge new territories. Carthage had to cede Spain and all of its island possessions to Rome. And though their North African homeland was spared, the Carthaginians had to give up all but ten of their warships and promise not to wage war on anyone without Rome's permission. That left the Romans in virtual control of two-thirds of the Mediterranean basin. The Greeks, who controlled the other third, now worried that, sooner or later, they would become Rome's next target. It turned out to be much sooner than anyone then imagined.

Roman Armies Overrun Greece

While the great conflicts between Rome and Carthage raged in the western Mediterranean sphere, most of the Greek kingdoms and city-states in the sea's eastern region watched with interest. Some of these states, like Athens and the island of Rhodes (off the coast of Asia Minor), were very ancient, having been founded well before Rome was. Others, especially the larger kingdoms, were fairly new, having formed in the wake of the bloody wars fought by the successors of the Greek conqueror Alexander the Great after his death in 323 B.C. Among the major players in the Greek sphere was the Macedonian kingdom, made up mostly of Macedonia (the region north of Greece) and portions of the Greek mainland.

Another was the Seleucid kingdom, encompassing most of what is now Iraq and Iran and most of Asia Minor. And the Ptolemaic kingdom consisted mainly of Egypt and parts of nearby Palestine. Smaller kingdoms were Pergamum (in western Asia Minor) and Epirus (in extreme northwestern Greece). Other important states included the Aetolian League (in western Greece) and Achaean League (in southern Greece), federations of cities that had banded together for mutual protection, and some powerful independent city-states, notably Rhodes, Athens, and Byzantium (near the entrance to the Black Sea). Modern scholars call these realms, as they existed in the post-Alexander era, Hellenistic, meaning

"Greek-like." The name reflects the fact that many of their societies consisted of various Eastern languages, customs, and ideas overlaid by a veneer of Greek ones.

A few of the Hellenistic Greeks had made the mistake of involving themselves, either for or against Rome, in the Second Punic War. Macedonia's King Philip V, who was worried about recent Roman encroachment into the Balkans, had allied himself with Hannibal. The Romans had countered this alliance by making some of their own alliances with Greeks, most prominently with the Aetolian League, which felt threatened by Philip. Thereafter, the Aetolians continually harassed Philip, keeping him from mounting a credible initiative against Rome while it was fighting Carthage.

More important in the long run, Rome's alliances in Greece had given it an inroad into that area, one the Roman military would soon begin to exploit. The immediate series of events that led to Rome's intervention in Greek affairs began early in 202 B.C., shortly before Hannibal's defeat at Zama. Philip and Antiochus III, ruler of the Seleucid kingdom, made a pact in which they planned to attack and partition (divide up) their chief rival, Ptolemaic Egypt. Rhodes and Pergamum viewed such a shift in the balance of power as a threat

A Roman general announces Greek independence. In reality this was an illusion.

to their own well-being and promptly appealed to Rome to thwart this sinister plan.

Perhaps fearing that a powerful alliance between Macedonia and Seleucia would threaten Roman interests as well as Greek ones, the Roman Senate sent envoys to Philip. They told him that he must under no circumstances attack any other Greek state; if he did so, he would face Rome's wrath. Philip was struck almost speechless by what he viewed as Roman arrogance and impudence. As Michael Grant points out:

This was a startling piece of interference, implying that Macedonia, one of the three great Greek empires, was, like Carthage, no longer entitled to have any foreign policy of its own; in other words, that it was a client of the Romans, taken . . . under their supervision. There had been hints of this doctrine before [in Roman policy] . . . but never before had it been applied to a major Greek power.[35]

Not surprisingly, therefore, Philip rebuffed the Romans, which turned out to be a grave miscalculation. His defiance, combined with the memory of his earlier interference in the Second Punic War, was

A Call for Greek Unity

Before 200 B.C., most Greeks did not yet appreciate the seriousness of the threat Rome posed to them. One exception was the orator Agelaus of Aetolia, who, in 213, made a speech (excerpted here from Polybius's Histories*) urging his fellow Greeks to unify.*

It would be best of all if the Greeks never went to war with one another, if they could regard it as the greatest gift of the gods for them to speak with one voice, and could join hands like men who are crossing a river; in this way they could unite to repulse the incursions of the barbarians and to preserve themselves and their cities. . . . We should consult one another and remain on our guard, in view of the huge armies which have been mobilized, and vast scale of the war [the Second Punic War] which is now being waged in the west. For it must already be obvious to all those who pay even the slightest attention to affairs of state that whether the Carthaginians defeat the Romans or the Romans the Carthaginians, the victors will by no means be satisfied with the sovereignty of Italy and Sicily, but will come here [to Greece], and will advance both their forces and their ambitions beyond the bounds of justice.

enough to provoke a Roman war declaration in 200 B.C. The Second Macedonian War, and ultimately Rome's dismemberment of Greece, had begun.

The Greek and Roman Systems Compared

Politically speaking, the war between Rome and Philip was significant because it marked the first time that the Roman army had launched an offensive into Greece. From a military standpoint, the conflict was noteworthy because it witnessed the first major clash between Europe's two most formidable and feared military systems. The Greeks still used the phalanx formation, which the Romans had long ago abandoned. However, in the intervening years the original Greek phalanx had undergone considerable changes. During the fourth century B.C. the Macedonian ruler Philip II had developed a much stronger and more lethal version of the formation. Generally known as the Macedonian phalanx, its basic structure resembled that of the traditional phalanx, as the soldiers stood in long lines, one behind the other. However, the members of the Macedonian phalanx did not carry the traditional six-foot-long thrusting spears. Instead, they wielded much longer spears, or battle pikes, called *sarissae*. The men in each succeeding rear rank held increasingly longer pikes, so that the tips of these weapons projected outward from the front of the phalanx. This created a tremendous mass of spear points

that looked something like a giant porcupine with its quills erect. (The men in the back rows held their *sarissae* upright to help block incoming enemy arrows and other missiles.) When the Macedonian phalanx moved forward, it was a truly frightening and deadly killing machine. In a now famous phrase, Polybius asserted, "Nothing can withstand the frontal assault of the phalanx so long as it retains its characteristic formation and strength."[36]

However, the incredible brute force of the Greek system ultimately could not match the flexibility and mobility of the Roman manipular system. An individual maniple or group of maniples was considerably less formidable than a Macedonian phalanx. Yet the Roman units could move back, forward, and around quickly at a commander's order, giving the Roman army a degree of maneuverability that the rigid phalanx lacked. "What then is the factor which enables the Romans to win the battle and causes those who use the phalanx to fail?" Polybius asked. His answer:

In war, the times and places for action are unlimited, whereas the phalanx requires one time and one type of ground only in order to produce its peculiar effect. . . . Its use requires flat and level ground which is unencumbered by any obstacles such as ditches, gullies, depressions, ridges, and water-courses, all of which are sufficient to hinder . . . such a formation. . . . If the enemy refuses to

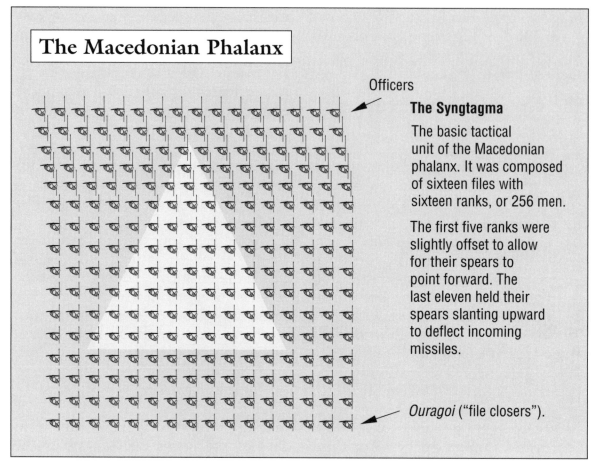

The Macedonian Phalanx

Officers

The Syngtagma

The basic tactical unit of the Macedonian phalanx. It was composed of sixteen files with sixteen ranks, or 256 men.

The first five ranks were slightly offset to allow for their spears to point forward. The last eleven held their spears slanting upward to deflect incoming missiles.

Ouragoi ("file closers").

come down [to meet it on level ground] . . . what purpose can the phalanx serve? . . . [Also], the phalanx soldier cannot operate either in smaller units or singly, whereas the Roman formation is highly flexible. Every Roman soldier, once he is armed and goes into action, can adapt himself equally well to any place or time and meet an attack from any quarter. . . . Accordingly, since the effective use of the parts of the Roman army is so much superior, their plans are much more likely to achieve success.[37]

The Slaughter at "Dog's Heads"

These "superior" qualities of the Roman army over its Greek counterpart showed themselves in short order. After three largely indecisive skirmishes fought in Greece, two in 200 B.C., the other in 198, the final, decisive battle of the conflict occurred in 197 at Cynoscephalae ("Dog's Heads"), a steep hill in central Greece. The fighting and its outcome signaled the reality that the Greek military system had become outdated. Philip's forces camped north of the hill, and the Roman army, led by Titus Quinctius Flamininus, camped only a few miles to the south. Neither was aware of the other's presence because of a dense morning fog. Just after dawn, each commander sent a small force of light-armed troops to occupy the summit, these

units ran into each other, and blows were struck. As the morning progressed, Philip and Flamininus rapidly mustered the main units of their armies and the conflict escalated in size and intensity.

While Philip was trying to assemble his phalanx, a complex and difficult task on

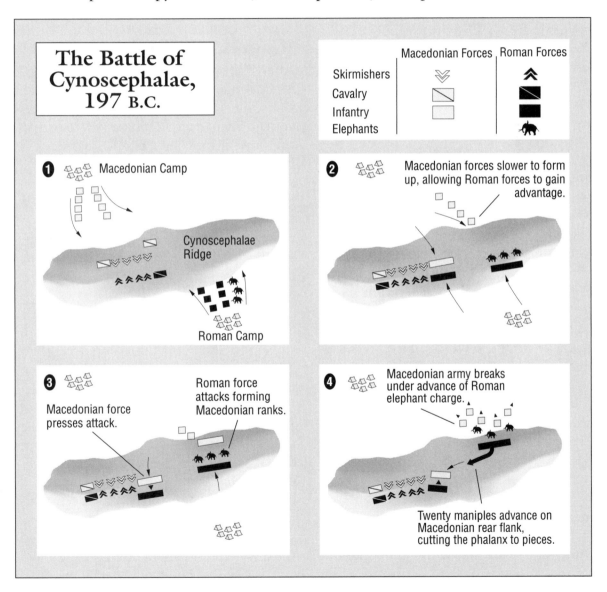

The Battle of Cynoscephalae, 197 B.C.

	Macedonian Forces	Roman Forces
Skirmishers		
Cavalry		
Infantry		
Elephants		

1 Macedonian Camp

Cynoscephalae Ridge

Roman Camp

2 Macedonian forces slower to form up, allowing Roman forces to gain advantage.

3 Macedonian force presses attack.

Roman force attacks forming Macedonian ranks.

4 Macedonian army breaks under advance of Roman elephant charge.

Twenty maniples advance on Macedonian rear flank, cutting the phalanx to pieces.

hilly terrain, Flamininus brought up his own infantry maniples and formed them into two groups, a left wing and right wing. Soon, one half of Philip's phalanx (constituting a smaller phalanx) managed to make it to the summit. Flamininus wisely decided to engage this unit with only half his army; he placed a row of battle elephants in front of his right wing, ordered that unit to hold its ground, and led his left wing against the enemy's partial phalanx. Though smaller than normal, this phalanx was still formidable, and it managed to drive the Roman left wing partway down the hill.

While this portion of the battle continued, Flamininus turned his attention to the other half of Philip's phalanx, which was still forming ranks at the base of the hill. The Roman commander led his own right wing, supported by the screen of elephants, in a devastating downhill charge that sent the Macedonians fleeing in all directions. At this same moment, at the rear of the Roman right wing, an unnamed Roman tribune acted on his own initiative. He led twenty maniples, made up mostly of veteran *triarii*, back up the hill and assaulted the rear of Philip's partial phalanx, which was still dueling Flamininus's left wing. Most of the Macedonian pikemen could not swing their bulky *sarissae* around to defend their backs. Surrounded, they were slaughtered in great numbers.

The scope of Philip's defeat stunned the Greek world. He lost eight thousand dead and five thousand captured while only about seven hundred Romans were killed. Flamininus's overwhelming victory confirmed the truth of Polybius's observation that the Roman army could adapt to changing situations as needed and outmaneuver the monolithic, inflexible phalanx. The war was over, and Greece's days were numbered.

Rome Versus Antiochus

After Philip sued for peace, Rome forced Macedonia to surrender most of its warships, pay large war reparations, and become a Roman ally. This last provision was the most important. The Romans could have killed or imprisoned Philip and dismantled his kingdom, but as had often been their custom in the past, they saw their defeated enemy as a potential partner who might prove useful in their struggles against another opponent. In this case, the other opponent was Antiochus and the Seleucid realm.

For the moment, the Romans made a show of giving the Greeks who had been subject to Macedonia their "freedom." In 196 B.C., at a major athletic competition held in Corinth, in southern Greece, Flamininus announced the so-called Act of Liberation. The problem was that most Greeks assumed this meant true independence, whereas in the Roman mind it implied a relationship between a patron and his clients. A Roman patron expected his clients to do him favors and vote as he instructed. Similarly, Rome now expected the Greeks it had liberated to pursue a foreign policy that benefited Roman interests.

Some Greeks were not so happy with the new arrangement. In particular, the Aetolians were disgruntled that Rome had not repaid them for their earlier help by letting them annex large portions of defeated Macedonia. So after Flamininus returned to Rome, they invited Antiochus to come to Greece and rid the region of Roman supporters and interests. In 192 B.C. the Seleucid king, who had greatly underestimated his enemy and overestimated his own abilities, answered the call and landed in Greece with an advance force of ten thousand troops.

The Romans wasted little time in dealing with Antiochus. In 191 B.C. the consul Acilius Glabrio arrived with about twenty thousand men and moved on the Seleucids, who fell back to the pass of Thermopylae, north of Delphi. This was the strategic site where a Spartan king, Leonidas, and a small band of Greeks had become legends by fighting to the death against an invading Persian army in 480 B.C. That defeat had occurred because a Persian force had taken a little-known mountain path and attacked the Greeks from behind; to avoid the same outcome, Antiochus had two thousand Aetolians guard the path. However, Glabrio sent four thousand legionaries against the Aetolians, dislodging them and clearing the way for a flanking movement identical to that of the Persians. When Antiochus's troops saw the Romans approaching their rear, they panicked. According to Livy:

Such sudden terror gripped them all that they cast away their arms and fled. . . . Out of the entire army, the only men to escape were the 500 who accompanied the king [who managed to escape]. . . . One hundred and fifty Romans fell in actual fighting, and there were not more than fifty casualties among those who defended themselves against the assault of the Aetolians.[38]

After this humiliating defeat, Antiochus fled all the way back to Asia Minor. Later the same year, a Roman fleet, aided by ships from Rhodes and Pergamum, engaged and defeated the Seleucid fleet near the coast of Asia Minor. Antiochus's admiral, who fled when he saw the Roman superiority in boarding tactics, lost ten ships sunk and thirteen captured; the Romans lost only a single vessel. The following year (190 B.C.) the Romans defeated the Seleucids at sea again.

A few months later, the Romans followed up these victories by sending a land army into Asia Minor. At Magnesia, a few miles inland from the Aegean coast, this army, numbering about thirty thousand, encountered Antiochus, who had amassed some sixty thousand infantry and twelve thousand cavalry. Though superior in numbers, the Seleucid soldiers were no match for the Roman legionaries. A panic among some of Antiochus's support troops spilled over into his phalanx, which then lost its cohesion under a terrific onslaught by the Roman maniples. The king

The Panic at Magnesia

In his great history of Rome (the following excerpts quoted in *Livy: Rome and the Mediterranean*), Livy describes the panic that swept the Seleucid ranks during the battle of Magnesia, which ended with the Roman army's crushing defeat of King Antiochus III. First, Livy reports, the Seleucid chariots, assailed with javelins and rocks, retreated in fear and confusion. Seeing this, the Seleucid auxiliaries, light-armed troops supporting the phalanx, "were terrified" and "they also turned and fled" toward the ranks of *cataphracti*, horsemen wearing metal armor. Some of the *cataphracti* "rushed away in flight," but "others were overwhelmed, burdened as they were by their armor and weapons."

Then the whole left flank [of the Seleucid army] gave ground, and . . . the panic reached as far as [the phalanx in] the center. There, as soon as the ranks were disordered and the use of the long spears-the Macedonians call them *sarissae*-was prevented because their comrades were rushing among them, the Romans legions advanced and hurled their spears into the disordered enemy."

lost as many as fifty thousand infantry and three thousand cavalry, compared to a mere 350 men killed on the Roman side.

Macedonia's Downfall

The disaster at Magnesia was so enormous that Antiochus surrendered immediately. The demands made by the Romans in the treaty were equally enormous. The Seleucids had to pay huge reparations (amounting to fifteen thousand talents) to Rome, give up all but ten of their warships, evacuate all of western Asia Minor, and promise never to attack any of Rome's allies. For their part in helping Antiochus, the Aetolians lost much territory and, more important, their independence.

These events made that concept—independence—seem more important than ever to large numbers of Greeks who resented Rome's presence in Greece. Anti-Roman factions grew larger in the cities of the Achaean League. And in Macedonia, Philip remained bitter over his former losses to the Romans and slowly and quietly began rebuilding his nation's military resources. Philip died in 179 B.C. before he could challenge Rome again; however, his son, Perseus, inherited not only the throne but also his father's enmity toward the Romans. Although Perseus made no overt actions against them, he began secretly to support the anti-Roman factions throughout the Greek sphere.

The Romans got wind of Perseus's activities and decided that he was a troublemaker who threatened to undermine their recent gains and ongoing policies in Greece. So they took the initiative and forced him into the Third Macedonian War (171–168 B.C.). The climax of the conflict came in 168, when the consul Lucius Aemilius Paullus faced off with Perseus at Pydna (near Greece's northeastern coast). As at Cynoscephalae, the flexibility of the Roman maniples proved vastly superior to the power of the Macedonian phalanx. As the battle opened, the phalanx drove the Romans back. But soon the increasing unevenness of the ground began to hinder the pikemen, and Paullus noticed that gaps were forming in the normally tight wall of the phalanx. He quickly divided several of his maniples in half and ordered these small groups into the gaps in the enemy formation. These acted like wedges, which drove the phalanx farther apart, and Roman troops surrounded each section of the disintegrating formation. In desperation, the Macedonian soldiers discarded their *sarissae*, which were now useless, and drew their swords, but with this weapon they were no match for the highly trained legionaries. Perseus lost about twenty-five thousand men, while Paullus's own losses numbered a hundred or fewer.

This time Rome was far less lenient with Macedonia than it had been following Philip's defeat thirty years before. Perseus was pulled from his throne, arrested, and transported to Rome, where he soon died in captivity. The Romans then dismantled his kingdom and partitioned it into four smaller "republics," which were clearly client states expected to do Rome's bidding. This turn of events "was an ominous landmark," as Grant puts it.

> Within the space of a single generation, the Greek world, before this dependent on the balance of power among three large empires, had been . . . transformed and ruined by the utter defeat of two of those states, one of which had been obliterated; and their place was filled by the Romans, who had entered the lands surrounding the Aegean and were there to stay.[39]

The Roman Lake

To demonstrate that they were indeed in Greece to stay, in the wake of Macedonia's demise the Romans methodically moved against other Greek states that might contemplate defiance. In the Achaean cities of southern Greece, the Romans rounded up and deported to Rome more than a thousand prominent citizens (among them the historian Polybius). These citizens were kept as hostages to ensure the good behavior of their homeland. Under Roman pressure, the Rhodians had to give up their possessions in Asia Minor, and Rome opened a rival market on the Aegean island of Delos that soon drew business away from Rhodes, ruining its economy. Meanwhile, in Epirus, Paullus, the victor of Pydna, sacked seventy towns and sold 150,000 of their inhabitants into slavery.

The Slaughter at Pydna

Here, from his history of Rome (quoted in Livy: Rome and the Mediterranean*), Livy describes the disintegration of the Macedonian phalanx at Pydna in 168 B.C.*

The most manifest cause of the [Roman] victory was the fact that there were many scattered engagements which first threw the wavering phalanx into disorder and then disrupted it completely. The strength of the phalanx is irresistible when it is close-packed and bristling with extended spears; but if by attacks at different points you force the troops to swing round their spears, unwieldy as they are by reason of their length and weight, they become entangled in a disorderly mass. . . . That is what happened in this battle, when the phalanx was forced to meet the Romans who were attacking in small groups, with the Macedonian line broken at many points. The Romans kept infiltrating their files [ranks of soldiers] at every place where a gap offered. . . . For a long time the phalanx was cut to pieces from the front, the flanks, and the rear. In the end, those who slipped from the hands of the Romans . . . met with destruction in a more horrible shape; for the [Macedonian] elephants [which by this time were in disarray] . . . trampled down the men . . . and crushed them to death.

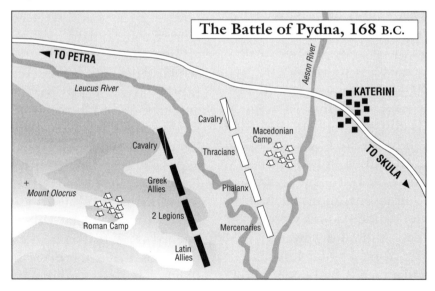

The Battle of Pydna, 168 B.C.

The final demonstration that the Roman army was in control of the Greek sphere came in the 140s B.C. Rome decided to abolish the four Macedonian republics it had recently created and annex the region outright as a Roman province. The Romans swiftly built a paved road, the Via Egnatia, through the area to better facilitate moving troops into Greece when needed. And as it turned out, they were needed almost right away. When the Romans intervened in a disagreement between the Achaean League and one of

Mummius watches as his men loot Corinth, one of Greece's greatest cities.

its members, Sparta, the Achaeans put up a fight. In 146 B.C. a Roman general, Lucius Mummius, crushed the rebels, dissolved the league, and utterly destroyed their capital, the once great city of Corinth. (Its inhabitants were sold into slavery and its art treasures were shipped to Rome.) The former Achaean cities now became part of the new Roman province of Macedonia.

In the span of a mere fifty-four years, the power of the Roman military had reduced the diverse, bustling, and rival but independent states of the Greek world to a flock of impotent, subservient Roman dependents. The last of the former great Hellenistic kingdoms—Ptolemaic Egypt—

had been spared for the moment. Yet it was nearly as impotent as the others, and for the brief remainder of its existence, it cowered in Rome's shadow. Egypt clearly did not want to share in the fate of Macedonia and Corinth, nor of unfortunate Carthage. In 146 B.C., the same year that Mummius destroyed Corinth, another Roman general completely eradicated Carthage at the close of the brief but brutal Third Punic War. The simultaneous demise of these two great cities, one in the east, the other in the west, underscored the stark reality of the day: The wide Mediterranean Sea, where once peoples from diverse lands had sailed and competed, had become a Roman lake.

Chapter 6

Julius Caesar Conquers Gaul

Having hammered most of the Greek states into submission during the second century B.C., Rome found itself in control of most of the Mediterranean's coastal regions. The three major European peninsulas jutting southward into that sea—Spain, Italy, and Greece—were in Roman hands. Yet most of the rest of Europe remained outside Roman control. The next major round of Roman conquests occurred during the following century when the famous politician and military general Julius Caesar led the Roman army into Gaul, a major bastion of the European heartland.

At the time, Gaul encompassed what is now France, Belgium, the Netherlands, western Switzerland, and the Po Valley of northern Italy. But the Romans separated Gaul into several regions. Cisalpine Gaul, constituting the Po Valley, had come under Rome's control shortly after the first Punic conflicts. Later, in 118 B.C., the Romans founded the colony of Narbonne in southern France. An area roughly two hundred miles wide surrounding the colony soon became a new province—Narbonese Gaul.

The rest of Gaul, stretching north of the Roman province, a region still largely unknown to Rome and well beyond its control, bore the name of Transalpine Gaul. This area, the one Caesar conquered, was inhabited by Celtic Gauls, the same group whose expedition into Italy during the fourth century B.C. had humiliated the Romans at Allia and briefly occupied

Rome. Loosely organized into about two hundred tribes, these Gauls had a total population of perhaps 10 to 15 million in Caesar's day. For a long time they had co-existed with the Greek and Roman cultures to their south. But the Gauls lacked the strong political and military organization for which Rome became renowned. During the years that Rome built great cities and many paved roads, the Gauls remained rural farmers and villagers with no large cities and only a few dirt roads. And while the Romans united Italy and acquired a Mediterranean empire, the Gauls remained largely disunited.

By conquering these peoples between 58 and 51 B.C., Caesar significantly expanded Rome's borders and influence.

More important, it was a bold northward thrust away from the Mediterranean sphere and into continental Europe. The Gallic lands rapidly became a huge new resource for Roman exploitation, including many fertile fields for growing grains, seemingly endless forests filled with valuable timber, not to mention gold and other metals and numerous other products. Some historians use the analogy of the opening of the Americas by Columbus and other later European explorers. In a like manner, Caesar opened up an enormous new world for Rome, one that promised to enrich and revitalize the old. And, as had been the case in earlier Roman conquests, the key to his success was the formidable Roman army, which he commanded with

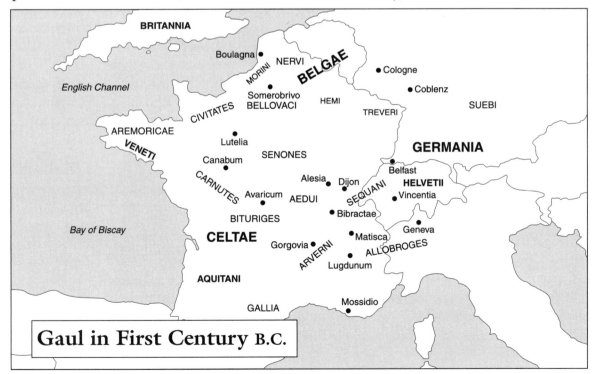

Gaul in First Century B.C.

a level of skill, authority, and sheer boldness that was rarely seen before or after.

Motivations for Conquest

To understand why and how Caesar launched these major military campaigns, one must first consider his political position in the years immediately preceding them. In 60 B.C. Caesar was a noted public figure, having served in a number of traditional government offices. But he had never commanded an army and had no troops under his control. To further his ambitions, therefore, Caesar shrewdly joined forces with his two chief political rivals, the noted military general Pompey, who did have the allegiance of an army, and the wealthy financier Crassus. Their powerful unofficial alliance, later called the First Triumvirate, allowed them to pool their resources and influence to ensure that Caesar would be elected consul for the year 59.

Caesar also looked beyond his consulship. When it ended, he reasoned, he would be more or less in the same position he had been before. For the moment, Pompey's troops protected Caesar and helped enforce his policies. But later, Pompey, who was also an ambitious man, might well withdraw this support or even use it *against* him. To maintain power

---

Caesar Describes Gaul

These are the famous opening lines of Julius Caesar's personal journal, the Commentary on the Gallic War *(Rex Warner's translation). Caesar briefly describes the major groups of peoples in Transalpine Gaul and emphasizes that some Gauls were involved in frequent warfare with German tribes on the far side of the Rhine River.*

The country of [Transalpine] Gaul consists of three separate parts, one of which is inhabited by the Belgae, one by the Aquitani, and one by the people whom we call "Gauls" but who are known in their own language as "Celts." The three peoples differ from one another in language, customs and laws. . . . The toughest soldiers come from the Belgae. This is because they are farthest away from the culture and civilized way of life of the Roman province [Narbonese Gaul]. . . . And they are also the nearest to the Germans across the Rhine and are continually waging war with them. . . . The Helvetii are the bravest tribe among the Gauls; [situated in Switzerland, they] too are in almost daily contact with the Germans, either fighting to keep them out of Gaul or launching attacks on them in their own country.

when no longer a consul, Caesar needed an army more loyal to him than to the state. One way to acquire such a force was to become governor of a province. For purposes of defense, provincial governors had access to troops and the authority to raise more. And in theory, an ambitious governor would be able to launch a military campaign, during which his men would become battle hardened and devoted to him.

While serving as consul, therefore, Caesar used his influence to become governor of both Cisalpine Gaul and Narbonese Gaul. When he took charge of these provinces in 58 B.C., he assumed command of roughly twenty-four thousand troops and quickly began raising more. He knew that his new goal—the conquest of Transalpine Gaul—was a major undertaking that would require the services of a large, well-trained army.

The Late Republican Army

Most of the Roman troops under Caesar's authority came from different backgrounds than those who had conquered Italy, Carthage, and the Greek lands. They were also equipped and organized differently. These differences were partly the result of the small, gradual changes that normally occur over time in any military organization. However, they were mainly due to large-scale reforms instigated by one of Rome's most distinguished political and military leaders, Gaius Marius (157–86 B.C.). Marius had served as consul an unprecedented seven times, six of

This modern engraving of the renowned general Julius Caesar is based on surviving busts.

them in the years 107 and 104 through 100 B.C. And in these years he had become a national hero by defeating two large Germanic tribes that had threatened to overrun northern Italy.

Marius used his tremendous power and influence to reshape what he saw as an outmoded Roman army into a more modern and efficient fighting force. In the past, he noted, only citizens who owned a certain amount of property were allowed to serve. This meant that many loyal and skilled men who would have made fine soldiers were excluded simply because they were poor. Also, those who did serve received few or no rewards. Recruits "were expected to supply their own equipment," historian Phillip Kildahl explains,

and, when war was over, to return to their homes without any pension or gratuity other than whatever booty had come their way. Because only the very wealthy could afford full armor, they were expected to do most of the fighting and to bear the heaviest burdens of the war. Those less wealthy who could afford only partial armor served in the second line of battle, and those so limited in funds that they could afford only a sword and shield were assigned to skirmishing.[40]

Seeing the inefficiency of this system, Marius made it his first order of business to eliminate all property qualifications and begin accepting volunteers from all social classes. On the one hand, this significantly increased the number of recruits; on the other, it changed the basic makeup of the army ranks. No longer mainly well-to-do men who saw military service as a necessary but unpleasant duty, most of the soldiers in the new army were volunteers who viewed military service as a career opportunity that could enrich and benefit their lives. In addition to regular pay, they could look forward to occasional bonuses and perhaps a small plot of land supplied by Marius when they retired.

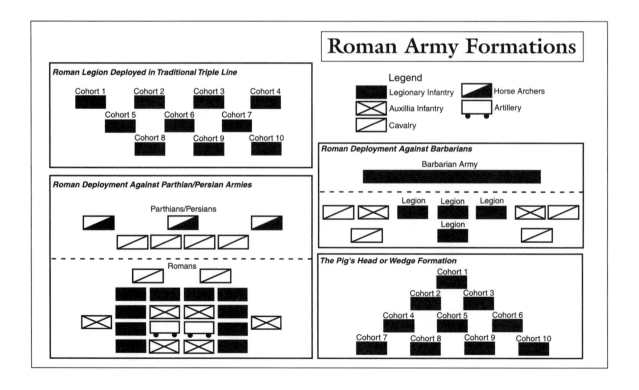

Roman Army Formations

Roman Legion Deployed in Traditional Triple Line

Cohort 1 Cohort 2 Cohort 3 Cohort 4
Cohort 5 Cohort 6 Cohort 7
Cohort 8 Cohort 9 Cohort 10

Roman Deployment Against Parthian/Persian Armies

Parthians/Persians

Romans

Legend
Legionary Infantry   Horse Archers
Auxillia Infantry   Artillery
Cavalry

Roman Deployment Against Barbarians

Barbarian Army

Legion Legion Legion
Legion

The Pig's Head or Wedge Formation

Cohort 1
Cohort 2 Cohort 3
Cohort 4 Cohort 5 Cohort 6
Cohort 7 Cohort 8 Cohort 9 Cohort 10

Marius also made important changes in weapons and armor. He introduced an improved version of the *pilum*, for instance. From his own experience he had noted that enemy soldiers often retrieved Roman javelins after they had been thrown and threw them back into the Roman lines. So the new version of the weapon was equipped with a wooden rivet that bent or broke on impact, which left the projectile useless to the enemy. Sometimes these javelins bent as they were penetrating enemy shields and were almost impossible to remove, rendering the shields useless as well. In addition, the Marian army, unlike the traditional manipular army, did not break down into four separate kinds of soldiers each with distinctive armor and weapons. The *velites, hastati, principes,* and *triarii* ceased to exist. And all legionaries wore cuirasses (often of mail, rows of iron rings either riveted or sewn together to form a protective shirt) and metal helmets and brandished the *scutum, gladius,* and two *pila.*

In another notable reform, Marius addressed the long, cumbersome baggage trains of mules that slowed down armies on the march. He trained his men to carry their own supplies, which, as Plutarch relates, earned them a nickname that came to be applied to dedicated Roman soldiers for generations to come:

Every man was compelled to carry his own baggage and to prepare his own meals. This was the origin of the expression "one of Marius's mules," applied later to any soldier who was a glutton for work and obeyed orders cheerfully and without grumbling.[41]

In addition, Marius sped up and completed a major organizational change that may already have been under way, namely the replacement of maniples with cohorts. A cohort was a unit consisting of about 480 men. It broke down further into six centuries of eighty men. An average legion had ten cohorts, or 4,800 men (although this number could vary somewhat under certain conditions). The introduction of cohorts did not significantly alter basic battlefield tactics. For one thing, each cohort, like a maniple, was an individual unit that could act on its own. Also, during battle the cohorts often formed three lines, as the maniples had. One line of cohorts could advance on the enemy while the cohorts of the other lines waited in reserve, as in manipular tactics.

However, the triple line of cohorts (*triplex acies*) was more effective than the old triple line of maniples, partly because the cohorts were fewer in number and easier to manage and arrange into strategic patterns. The most common arrangement of cohorts was four in the front line, three in the second, and three in the rear. But other combinations were used when a commander deemed them appropriate. For example, the "pig's head," consisting of one cohort in front, two behind it, three in the third row, and the other four in the rear, was an enormous wedge that could slice through and disrupt a solid bank of enemy soldiers.

Caesar's First Battle

The army that Caesar took charge of in Gaul, therefore, was a Marian-style force composed of cohorts made up of standard legionaries who all used the same weapons and basic tactics. As such, it was superior in most ways to the forces of the Celtic Gauls he would soon face on the battlefield. Most Celtic warriors of Caesar's era fought naked from the waste up, weather permitting (although nobles and others who could afford it sometimes wore mail). They usually donned long leather pants and leather shoes. They also sported long hair, which before battle they caked with clay, making it stand up on end. Like their ancestors at Allia, the Celts painted themselves with tattoos to make themselves appear more frightening.

In actual battle, Gallic commanders placed their best warriors in the front line and/or in the center. It is unclear whether these fighters began a battle standing in well-ordered lines, but even if they did, it appears that they quickly fell into an unorganized mass once the battle got under way. This was a definite disadvantage when facing the well-organized Roman army. Another drawback was the fact that at close quarters the Gauls' large, heavy swords and small shields were not very effective against the thrusting swords and larger, more protective shields of the Roman legionaries.

These differences in weapons and fighting techniques were only too obvious in the first major battle Caesar fought in his Gallic campaigns. Early in 58 B.C. the Helvetii, a populous Gallic tribe hailing from western Switzerland, began a mass migration that threatened to overrun Caesar's province of Narbonese Gaul. With a force of four legions, he attacked the tribesmen near the Saone River, just north of the province. Caesar himself described what happened when the opposing armies clashed:

> Hurling their javelins . . . our men easily broke up the enemy's mass formation and, having achieved this, drew their swords and charged. In the fighting, the Gauls were seriously hampered because several of their overlapping shields were often pierced by a single [Roman] javelin; the iron head would bend and they could neither get it out nor fight properly with their left arms. Many of them, after a number of vain efforts at disentangling themselves, preferred to drop their shields and fight with no protection for their bodies. In the end, the wounds and the toll of battle were too much for them and they began to retire.[42]

Campaigns in Northern Gaul

Caesar's defeat of the Helvetii forced the tribe to return to its homeland in the Alpine foothills. Perhaps as many as sixty thousand Gauls had been slain. Caesar claimed a number more than four times as large in the personal journal he kept during these years. This was almost surely an exaggeration to impress the Roman populace, who eagerly read the journal in installments he sent back.

Hearing of the Helvetii's demise, numerous tribes in central Gaul quickly sent ambassadors to Caesar, offering to sign treaties of peace and friendship. One of the strongest tribes in the region, the Aedui, even offered to become Roman allies. The Aedui and others then urged Caesar to fight their perpetual enemy, the Germans, who dwelled beyond the Rhine River, the unofficial boundary separating Gaul and the Germanic lands to the east. Still eager to gain battle experience, in the autumn of 58 B.C. Caesar defeated a large German army, which retreated in disarray. The victory was so decisive that the Rhine frontier remained quiet for several years afterward.

Next, Caesar moved against the Belgae, a group of tribes inhabiting the remote northern reaches of Gaul. These Belgian tribes had many fine warriors, but they failed to unite against the encroaching Romans. So Caesar was able to pick them off or make treaties with them one by one. The strongest resistance in the region came from the reclusive and extremely fierce Nervii, whom Caesar described this way:

No traders ever came into their country because they did not allow wine to be imported or any other luxury, in the belief that indulgences of this sort make men feeble-spirited and lacking in courage. A fierce people and extremely courageous, they were very bitter in their denunciations of the other Belgae for having forgotten the traditional courage of their race and given in to Rome. As to themselves, they had declared that they would never send envoys to us and never accept any kind of peace.[43]

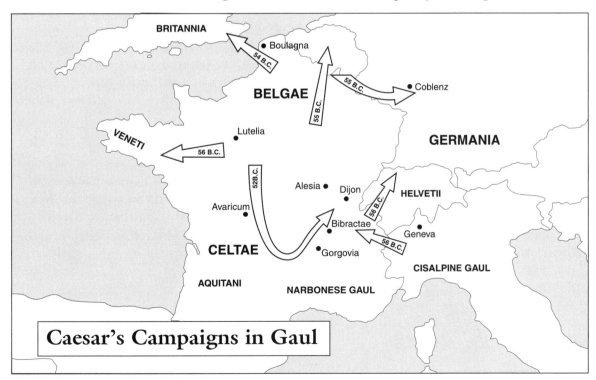

Caesar's Campaigns in Gaul

In a hard-fought battle in which the Nervii launched a surprise attack on Caesar's camp, the Romans were, with great difficulty, triumphant. According to Caesar, of the sixty thousand attackers, only some five hundred survived.

Fighting for Caesar's Glory

In the battle against the Nervii, as in many other subsequent conflicts, Caesar displayed uncommon courage, fighting prowess, and leadership skills. He earned both the respect and admiration of his men while grooming them into a truly formidable fighting force devoted more to him than to Rome itself. He improved the quality of their weapons, introduced new and more effective training methods for new recruits, and, perhaps most important, doubled the soldiers' pay.

Caesar also took what appeared to be a sincere interest in his men's daily needs and often engaged ordinary grunts, as well as officers, in meaningful conversations. "His ability to secure the affection of his men and to get the best out of them was remarkable," Plutarch wrote.

Soldiers who in other campaigns had not shown themselves to be any bet-

Attack of the Nervii

One of the more hair-raising episodes in Julius Caesar's Gallic campaigns was the day he and his men were attacked by the Nervii, a tribe whose warriors fought with unusual bravery and ferocity. This description of the opening of the battle comes from Caesar's war commentaries (Rex Warner's translation).

The infantry of the Nervii, full of confidence, were . . . drawn up in battle order under cover of the woods. . . . They suddenly rushed out of the woods in full force and charged down on our cavalry, whom they brushed aside. . . . They then swept down to the river, moving at such an incredible speed that to us it looked as though they were at the edge of the woods, in the river, and on top of us all in the same moment. With the same extraordinary speed, they swarmed up the opposite hill toward our camp. . . . I had everything to do at once—hoist the flag (which was the signal for a call to arms), sound the trumpet for action . . . form the troops up in battle order, address them, [and] give the signal for attack. As the enemy was practically upon us, there was simply not time to do most of these things, but . . . from their knowledge of previous battles [our men] were able to dispense with orders and judge on their own what should be done.

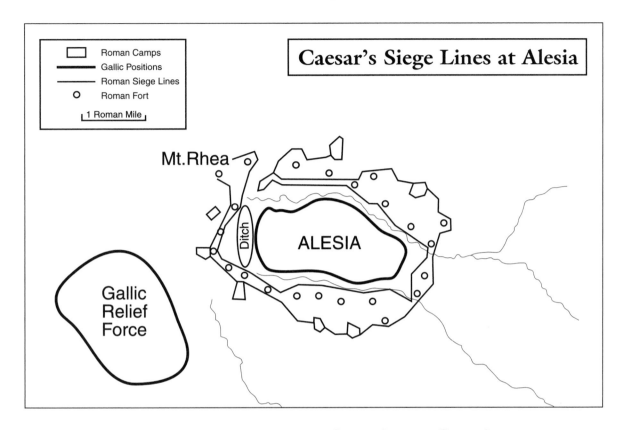

ter than the average became irresistible and invincible and ready to confront any danger, once it was a question of fighting for Caesar's honor and glory. . . . It was Caesar himself who inspired this passion for distinction among his men. . . . He showed that there was no danger which he was not willing to face, no form of hard work from which he excused himself.[44]

The troops' devotion to their commander became so great that, as Michael Grant puts it, "Their fatherland was Caesar's camp, and their patriotism was loyalty to Caesar."[45]

Opening a Continent

With this remarkable fighting force at his disposal, Caesar managed to defeat or at least intimidate and pacify most of the tribes of Transalpine Gaul by the spring of 56 B.C. Then, without warning, trouble erupted in Brittany (the coastal region of northwestern France). The Veneti, a maritime tribe with a large fleet of ships, seized some of Caesar's officers and made other threatening moves. Caesar hurried to Brittany and, with the aid of one of his more gifted officers, Decimus Albinus, soundly defeated the Veneti.

Caesar now found himself camped on the English Channel with several legions and numerous ships. He knew that beyond

The Siege Works at Alesia

When Julius Caesar was besieging Alesia, groups of Gallic warriors often harassed Roman soldiers guarding the perimeter. So Caesar ordered the construction of ramparts, ditches, and booby traps, as he relates in his war commentaries (Rex Warner's translation).

Tree trunks or very stout branches were cut down and the ends were stripped of bark and sharpened; long trenches, five feet deep, were dug and into these the stakes were sunk and fastened at the bottom so that they could not be torn up, while the top part projected above the surface. There were five rows of them in each trench, fastened and interlaced together in such a way that anyone who got among them would impale himself on the sharp points. The soldiers called them "tombstones." In front of these, arranged in diagonal lines forming quincunxes, we dug pits three feet deep and tapering downward toward the bottom. Smooth stakes as thick as a man's thigh, hardened by fire and with sharp points, were fixed in these pits and set so as not to project more than about three inches from the ground. To keep them firmly in place, the earth was trodden down hard to a depth of one foot and the rest of the pit was filled with twigs and brushwood so as to conceal the trap. These traps were set in groups, each of which contained eight rows three feet apart. The men called them "lilies" from their resemblance to that flower. In front of these was another defensive device. Blocks of wood a foot long with iron hooks fixed in them were buried underneath the surface and thickly scattered all over the area. They were called "spurs" by the soldiers.

Caesar's siege works at Alesia, with guard towers, an earthen mound topped by a wooden stockade, and many booby traps.

this waterway loomed the mysterious island of Britain, which was fabled for its gold, tin, and pearls. So twice—first in 55 B.C. and again during the following year—he crossed the channel and fought the natives, who were Celtic cousins of the Gauls. Both forays were unsuccessful, however, partly because Caesar did not have the large quantities of men and supplies needed to both conquer and hold so large a country and partly because storms wrecked many of his ships.

Back in Gaul, in 52 B.C. Caesar had to contend with an enormous uprising led by Vercingetorix, war chief of the Arverni tribe, the greatest military leader the Gauls ever produced. After meeting Vercingetorix in open battle, Caesar besieged him in his fortress of Alesia (in north-central Gaul). There, huge numbers of Gallic reinforcements surrounded the Romans. But in an enormous battle lasting four days, Caesar was victorious. By the end of 51 B.C., Rome was firmly in control of almost all of Transalpine Gaul.

On the one hand, these bold and bloody events established Caesar as Rome's leading political and military figure. Soon afterward, he fought and won a civil war that rocked the known world. However, as Michael Grant points out, the consequences of Caesar's Gallic conquests

went very far beyond any considerations limited to his personal career. The area now annexed was twice the size of contemporary Italy and far more populous than Spain. . . . Caesar

Soldiers of Caesar's army take a well earned break during one of the Gallic campaigns.

had changed the whole idea and nature of Roman dominion. It had ceased to be merely a Mediterranean maritime strip, and had become a vast land empire of which Gaul was to be the hinge. The conqueror had opened up the continent to his peculiar brand of civilization. He had laid the foundations of modern France. He had ended the prehistory of Western Europe and started its history, of which we are the heirs.[46]

Rome's Early Imperial Conquests

The end product of centuries of rigorous military reforms and honed by numerous hard-fought campaigns, the Roman army of Julius Caesar's day was the most formidable war machine in the known world. But there was a major inherent weakness in the system. Namely, the government had neglected to develop a policy of rewarding the soldiers with substantial pensions and land when they retired. Meeting this need, the most powerful generals—men like Marius and Caesar—used their own considerable wealth and influence to secure such benefits for their men. The result was that many soldiers increasingly came to show more allegiance to their generals than to the state.

Having amassed what amounted to personal armies, this new breed of military strongmen, with names like Sulla, Pompey, Caesar, Octavian, and Antony, faced off in a series of devastating civil wars. The republican state, led by the Senate, could not mount an effective defense. Drained of its resources and stripped of its military support, it sagged and then collapsed over the course of two or three decades. The fatal climax came in 31 B.C. when Octavian, Caesar's great-nephew and adopted son, defeated the last of his rivals in a great sea battle at Actium in western Greece.

Yet the fall of the Republic did not mark the end of Rome, its remarkable army, or its desire to use this instrument of power to conquer and rule others. The triumphant

Octavian now had control of that instrument, as well as the state, and he shrewdly used both to his advantage. Renamed Augustus, "the revered one," in 27 B.C. by the now largely impotent Senate, he consolidated the powers of most of the old republican offices in his own hands. Though he never called himself an emperor, he was in fact the first ruler of the long-lived political entity known as the Roman Empire. Under Augustus and several of his immediate successors, the Roman army, now an imperial force, resumed its role as a tool for expanding Roman territory and interests.

Augustus's New Standing Army

The new imperial army was, of necessity, different from the late republican army in a number of ways. First and foremost was the matter of maintaining the loyalty of the troops. Augustus realized that he would not stay in power long if the soldiers swore allegiance to individual generals, as had happened so often in the recent past. It was imperative, therefore, that he reform the military to ensure that the men would be completely loyal to him and his new autocratic government.

Octavian Becomes Augustus

In his history of Rome, the second-century Roman historian Dio Cassius gives this explanation of the derivation of the title Augustus, which Octavian received in 27 b.c.

When Octavian had finally put his plans into effect, the name Augustus was conferred on him by the Senate and the people. At the time when they wished to give him some title of special importance . . . Octavian had set his heart strongly on being named Romulus [Rome's founder]. But when he understood that this aroused suspicions that he desired the kingship [because Romulus had also been Rome's first king], he abandoned his efforts to obtain it and adopted the title of Augustus, as signifying that he was something more than human, since indeed all the most precious and sacred objects are referred to as *augusta*. For this reason, when he was addressed in Greek he was named *Sebastos*, meaning an august individual; the word is derived from the passive form of the verb *sebazo*, "I revere." Through this process, the power of the people and the Senate was wholly transferred into the hands of Augustus, and it was from this time that a monarchy, strictly speaking, was established.

Part of Augustus's solution to this problem was to retain and expand on the Marian concept of a professional army of volunteers. Obviously, career men who enlisted by choice were more likely to support the establishment than a renegade general. Second, Augustus ordered the soldiers to swear an oath to him as their supreme commander once each year. Making them renew the vow over and

This statue of the first emperor, Augustus, was found at Prima Porta, near Rome.

over helped to reinforce the concept that they owed their fidelity to the state, not to their generals. The emperor also remedied the problem of military pensions. In his new system, the soldiers received grants of land on retirement. They also received periodic bonuses on top of their regular pay before retirement so that it became almost impossible for a renegade general to buy their loyalty.

Augustus also altered the number of soldiers in his new army and the duration of their service. At the end of the civil wars, about five hundred thousand men were in arms, in his view far too many to pay, feed, and keep busy and loyal during peacetime. So he reduced the size of the military from sixty or seventy legions to twenty-eight, or a little more than 150,000 men. Moreover, he turned this smaller force into a full-time standing army. He raised the term of service from a few years (usually six) to sixteen years, plus four years in an on-call reserve force; later, he upped it to twenty years of initial service, plus five on-call. Thus, though the imperial government had fewer troops at its disposal, these men made up a more reliable and professional force.

The full-time imperial troops were also better trained than ever. Military training in the republican period had been arduous but of fairly brief duration since most soldiers had served relatively short hitches. Under the Empire, by contrast, training was truly grueling. New recruits had to take part in exhausting parade drills twice a day until they were able to cover twenty-four miles in just five hours while wearing full armor. Then they marched all day, day after day, for weeks, carrying a pack loaded with sixty pounds of weapons, tools, and rations. The recruits were also instructed in building marching camps, riding horses, and swimming. As for weapons training, the third-century Roman writer Vegetius says that at first the men used wooden swords and wicker shields, all double the weight of the real versions:

> With these they were made to practice at the stakes both morning and afternoon. . . . A stake was planted in the ground by each recruit, in such a manner that it projected six feet in height and could not sway. Against this stake the recruit practiced . . . just as if he were fighting a real enemy. . . . He gave ground, he attacked, he assaulted, and he assailed the stake with all the skill and energy required in actual fighting.[47]

In other drills, the recruits threw spears, took part in forced marches and long runs in armor, and practiced jumping and felling trees. Eventually, they assembled in an open field and practiced shaping the various battle formations of cohorts until they could do so quickly and precisely. Finally, they fought mock battles with real weapons (although the points of their swords and *pila* were covered to reduce the incidence of serious injuries).

Augustus Expands the Realm

In theory, Augustus's new streamlined and professional army was a tool mainly for maintaining order and defending the realm against attack. Yet he soon began to use it as many republican leaders had—to implement aggressive foreign policy and expand the realm. At least part of this policy was motivated by what the emperor and many other Roman leaders perceived as national security issues. In the early years of Augustus's reign, Rome's northern border was an uneven frontier that ran west to east from eastern Gaul, through the central and northern Alps, and then dipped southeastward along the upper boundary of Illyricum (the name given to Illyria when it became a province). In the mountains and forests lying beyond this ill-defined border dwelled the tribal peoples whom the

Modern reenactors play Roman legionaries training with wooden swords and wicker shields.

Drusus the Elder leads his troops in a successful campaign against the Germans in 15 B.C.

Augustus's view, a more distant, more easily defended, and therefore safer barrier against the barbarians would be the Danube River, located about 150 miles north of the existing border. So in 25 B.C. imperial forces moved northward into the Alps and began securing the valleys and passes. To make sure these areas remained pacified, the soldiers built roads and established military colonies in the conquered areas.

In 15 B.C. the emperor sped up these efforts by putting his two stepsons, Nero Tiberius Drusus (called Tiberius) and Nero Claudius Drusus (called Drusus the Elder), in charge. Both capable generals, they soon reached the Danube, which became the Empire's new northern border, per Augustus's original plan. Some of the territory acquired in these conquests went to enlarging the existing province of Illyricum; the rest was divided up into four new provinces—Raetia, Noricum, Pannonia, and Moesia.

Romans referred to collectively as Germans. (Because the Germans had no cities, paved roads, or high culture, the Romans also called them barbarians.) The Germans periodically raided Gaul and other Roman lands. And Augustus felt that their presence so near the Italian homeland was dangerous and unacceptable.

Therefore, the imperial government initiated campaigns designed to push the frontiers farther northward and eastward. In

Though Augustus had achieved his goal of expanding to the Danube, he was apparently no longer satisfied with what now seemed rather modest gains. Some evidence suggests that he began to envision a much more ambitious goal, perhaps the conquest and Romanization of all of northern Europe. At the least, his new plan provided for a bold thrust into the lands lying between the Rhine, Danube, and Elbe Rivers, the very heartland of Germany. In 12 B.C. the widely popular Drusus the Elder crossed the Rhine and in only three years subdued the tribes in this key region.

It is entirely feasible that Roman forces, which at this point seemed unstoppable, could have gone on to capture most of the rest of Germany in the next few years. However, this plan was now derailed by some serious setbacks. First, shortly after his triumphant campaigns, Drusus fell from his horse and died, an event that plunged Romans everywhere into mourning. Thanks to his brother, Tiberius, who kept troops in the region, the German frontier remained relatively quiet for a while. It was so quiet, in fact, that Augustus decided

it was time to organize the area into a new province. To carry out this assignment, he sent a former consul named Publius Quinctilius Varus, who turned out to be an extremely poor choice. Varus was a conceited, tactless man and a heavy-handed administrator. Instead of fostering good relations with the conquered Germans so as to ease them into the Roman fold, he insulted, abused, and overtaxed them.

Thirsting for revenge, the natives eventually struck back. In A.D. 9 in the dense Teutoburg Forest (about eighty miles east of the Rhine), a large force of German warriors surrounded, ambushed, and annihilated Varus and the fifteen thousand troops under his command. According to the first-century A.D. Roman historian Suetonius:

Varus and his men fight to the death against impossible odds in the Teutoburg Forest. After the ambush, the Romans ended their campaign to Romanize the Germans.

Three legions with their general and all their officers and auxiliary forces, and the general staff, were massacred to a man. When news reached Rome, Augustus . . . took the disaster so deeply to heart that he left his hair and beard untrimmed for months; he would often beat his head on a door, shouting: "Quinctilius Varus, give me back my legions!" and always kept the anniversary as a day of deep mourning.[48]

Not only was it impossible for Varus to give the legions back, Augustus could not easily replace them. Despite the over-all prosperity of the realm and the emperor's considerable personal wealth, it would have been prohibitively expensive to raise, outfit, and train three entire legions at once. A huge empire-wide raise in taxes might have done it, but the resentment and unrest such a move would likely have caused made it out of the question. For many years to come, therefore, the Roman army simply made do with twenty-five instead of twenty-eight legions.

The Invasion of Britain

With such reduced forces at his disposal, Augustus probably felt that he

---

Germany's Resources

In this tract from his Germania, *the Roman historian Tacitus describes the countryside and natural resources of southern Germany, the region Augustus conquered with an army commanded by his stepsons, Tiberius and Drusus the Elder.*

The appearance of the country differs considerably in different parts; but in general it is covered either by bristling forests or by foul swamps. It is wetter on the side that faces Gaul, windier on the side of Noricum and Pannonia. A good soil for cereal crops, it will not grow fruit trees. It is well-provided with livestock; but the animals are mostly undersized, and even the cattle lack the handsome heads that are their natural glory. It is the mere number of them that the Germans take pride in; for these are the only form of wealth they have, and are much prized. Silver and gold have been denied them, whether as a sign of divine favor or divine wrath, I cannot say. Yet I would not positively assert that there are no deposits of silver or gold in Germany, since no one has prospected for them. The natives take less pleasure than most people do in possessing and handling these metals. . . . Those who live on the frontiers nearest us, however, do value gold and silver for their use in commerce, being quick to recognize and pick out certain of our coin-types.

---

was overreaching with his current German policy. So he withdrew the army from the Elbe back to the Rhine and Danube, allowing the natives to regain control of the area and, in effect, writing off Germany as a loss. His earlier gains south of the Danube still stood, however. And he enjoyed a series of successes on other fronts. These included adding new territory in Roman Spain; creating the new province of Lusitania (now Portugal); bringing Egypt, the last of the great Hellenistic states, into the realm; and significantly expanding Roman interests in North Africa, Asia Minor, and Palestine.

Thanks to these gains, Augustus's successors ruled a much larger and more diverse realm than the one that existed in Julius Caesar's day. Also, these rulers inherited from the first emperor the most powerful standing army the world had yet seen, a potent tool they could use to further their own individual foreign policies. Conquests continued in the century following Augustus's death (in A.D. 14), therefore. But in general they were more sporadic and on a smaller scale than those of the past.

The biggest and most important military campaign of the first century A.D. was the conquest of Britain. Ever since

The Caledonians of Britain, also called Picts, used elaborate body paint to look fearsome.

Caesar's brief forays to that island during the preceding century, Roman leaders had dreamed of returning. It fell to Claudius, the fourth emperor, to make that dream a reality. In A.D. 43 he sent an army of some forty thousand men across the English Channel. Commanded by a skilled general, Aulus Plautius, the Romans captured Camulodunum (modern Colchester) and rapidly transformed the southern part of the island into a new province—Britannia. After becoming governor, Plautius, who ruled from Camulodunum, extended Roman control farther toward the north and west. And his successor, Ostorius Scapula, seized sections of what is now Wales.

A temporary setback in this process of expansion occurred in 60, when the Iceni tribe, commanded by the warrior queen Boudicca, led a bloody rebellion of the tribes living in Roman territory. The natives managed to kill many Romans. But fresh contingents of the Roman army soon arrived and beat the rebels into submission.

Victory at Mons Graupius

Not long after crushing the revolt, the Romans moved the provincial capital to Londinium (London). From this base, a new governor, Gnaeus Julius Agricola, one of the finest military generals of the era, launched a new round of conquests. Agricola, who was also the father-in-law of the great Roman historian Tacitus, com-

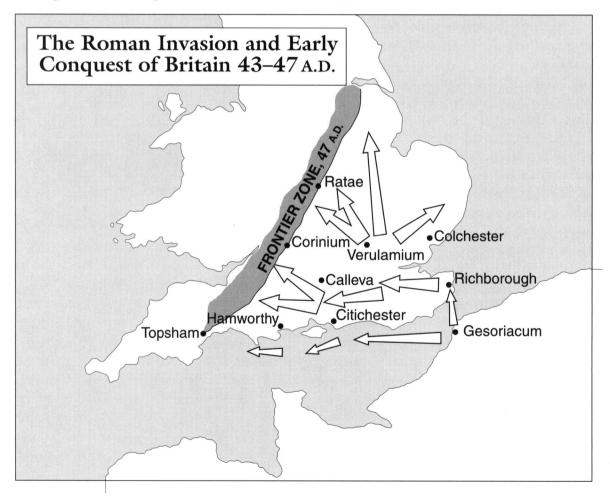

The Roman Invasion and Early Conquest of Britain 43–47 A.D.

FRONTIER ZONE, 47 A.D.

Ratae

Corinium

Verulamium

Colchester

Calleva

Richborough

Citichester

Hamworthy

Topsham

Gesoriacum

pleted the subjugation of Wales. Then the general turned north and invaded Caledonia (Scotland). In 84 Agricola enjoyed a great victory over the Caledonians at Mons Graupius (the location of which is disputed). He later described the encounter in considerable detail to Tacitus, who included the information in a book about his illustrious relative; this firsthand account provides valuable insights into how a Roman army of that era operated in the field.

Like other Roman armies of the day, Agricola's broke down into roughly equal numbers of regular Roman troops, who were citizens, and auxiliary troops, who were noncitizens from various Roman provinces. Both groups were armed and trained more or less the same. Agricola placed his auxiliary infantry cohorts, which numbered eight thousand men, in the front ranks. His cavalry, numbering three thousand, guarded the flanks, with fifteen hundred on the left and the same number on the right. Behind these frontline troops stood perhaps eight thousand to nine thousand regular legionaries, who formed a reserve force. "If the auxiliaries should be repulsed," Tacitus writes, "the legions could come to their rescue."[49] (These figures do not count light-armed skirmishers, who may have numbered a thousand or more.)

Tacitus says that there were about thirty thousand Caledonians arrayed in front of the Romans. "Their front line was on the plain, but the other ranks seemed to mount up the sloping hillside in close-packed tiers."[50] This arrangement, which clearly showed off the natives' greater numbers,

was a purposeful attempt to intimidate the Romans. Meanwhile, in the flat space between the opposing armies, the Celtic chariots, per custom, rode back and forth in a pre-battle show, their warriors screaming threats at the enemy soldiers. When Agricola saw how badly he was outnumbered, he thinned the ranks of his auxiliaries so that his battle line would be wider. That way, there was less chance of being outflanked.

The battle opened with skirmishers from both sides hurling javelins into the enemy lines. This tactic was ineffective overall. The Romans were heavily armored, and their shields provided sufficient cover from missile weapons. Likewise, Tacitus relates, the Caledonian infantrymen "showed both steadiness and skill" in deflecting the Roman *pila* "with their huge swords or catching them on their little shields."[51]

After the skirmishers retired from the field, Agricola ordered his auxiliary infantry units forward. Following their training, they hurled their light *pila* at a distance of about a hundred feet from the enemy, and then, only a few seconds later, followed up with their heavier ones. Finally, they drew their swords, closed the remaining gap between themselves and the enemy, and smashed into the Caledonian front ranks. With their larger, more cumbersome swords, smaller shields, and lack of armor, the natives were unable to match the Romans, who swiftly pushed them backward and partway up the hill.

At this point, the Caledonians tried to take advantage of their superior numbers by outflanking the attacking enemy. An unknown number of warriors from the hillside swarmed down and tried to get behind the Romans. However, Agricola "had expected just such a move," according to Tacitus. The Roman commander "threw in their path four squadrons of cavalry which he was keeping in hand for emergencies."[52] These horsemen surrounded the Caledonians who had moved off the hill, killed many of them, and drove off many more. Then, following Agricola's orders, the horsemen continued on, rode up the hill, and began to envelop the enemy's rear.

Seeing that they were steadily becoming surrounded, many of the Caledonians grew fearful and their ranks began to fall into chaos. Some fled over the hilltop while others, in desperation, threw themselves into the Roman ranks and certain death. Having won the battle, Tacitus says, the Romans chased down the survivors, a pursuit that "went on till night fell and our soldiers were tired of killing."[53] About 10,000 Caledonians were killed, compared to about 360 Romans.

Master of the World

It is almost certain that Agricola could have successfully completed the conquest of Scotland. However, for reasons that are unclear, the reigning emperor, Domitian, did not see fit to commit the army to this task. In the next few years, therefore, the Romans pulled back from the Scottish highlands and established a frontier on their southern edge. (It was here that a later em-peror, Hadrian, would erect his famous defensive wall stretching for seventy-three miles east to west across northern Britain.)

In the years that followed, the Roman army facilitated still more territorial expansion. Chief among these conquests were those of the emperor Trajan, who ascended the throne in 98. In 101 he launched an invasion of Dacia, the rugged, mountainous region located north of the Danube in what is now eastern Hungary. Trajan quickly subdued the area, but a local rebellion that erupted in 105 forced him to lead a larger army into Dacia. This time the emperor completely pacified the region and made it a Roman province.

Trajan also carved out new provinces in Arabia (the region southeast of Syria), Armenia (east of Asia Minor), and Mesopotamia (between Syria and the Tigris River). When he died in 117, the Roman realm was larger than it had ever been. It stretched from the Atlantic Ocean in the west to Mesopotamia in the east, and from North Africa in the south to north-central Britain in the north, about 3.5 million square miles in all. More than 100 million people were either Roman citizens or Roman subjects. Rome's political and economic ambitions, supported by its tough, skilled, relentless army, had won it mastery of most of the known world. The most important question that no one was then asking was: How long could the Romans maintain that control?

Epilogue
The Roman Army's Decline

In Trajan's time, no one realized that a major turning point had taken place, namely that the Roman Empire had reached its zenith in size and power. The reality was that Trajan's conquests marked the effective end of Rome's foreign gains, the close of a long era in which the Roman army was almost always on the offensive somewhere. In the years that followed, the military steadily reverted to a defensive mode as the Empire faced increasing threats to its integrity and began to lose the many territories it had gained.

Threats to the Borders

By far the greatest of these outside threats came from the Germanic tribes of central and northern Europe. These were the peoples whom Augustus had failed to conquer and absorb at the dawn of the Empire. Like a river that slowly creates an expanding lake behind a high dam, over the years the Germans gained in numbers and strength and all the while looked with envious eyes on the Roman lands to their south. The human river began to spill over the dam during the second century. Not long after ascending the throne in 161, the emperor Marcus Aurelius had to deal with numerous serious incursions by German tribes. He managed to keep them at bay, but only at a great cost in human and material resources.

What is more, the fix proved temporary, as the Germans launched new attacks on the northern borders during the following century. In the 230s they penetrated the Danube frontier, which became an almost perpetual battleground. Some even managed to make it into northern Italy before the emperor Gallienus stopped them.

Meanwhile, Rome's eastern borders also came under attack. In 253 Shapur I, a Persian ruler of the Sassanian dynasty, invaded several of Rome's eastern provinces. The emperor Valerian (253–260) responded, but Shapur took him prisoner during a meeting held under a flag of truce. Emboldened, Shapur then pushed deeper into Roman territory.

Part of the reason that these invaders enjoyed so much success was that the Roman military was no longer the efficient, loyal machine it had once been. Indeed, by this time the army had grown less disciplined and reliable than it had been in the days of Trajan and Marcus Aurelius. Making matters worse, at the height of the crises of the third century the government had serious financial troubles, which made it difficult to pay the troops regularly. This contributed to a reversion to the old practice of army units swearing allegiance to their generals. Moreover, many of these generals wasted precious time and resources fighting one another at the same time that they were attempting to drive back the invaders.

The Beginning of the End

Eventually, a series of tough, competent Roman military leaders did manage to push back the intruders and restore order to the realm. The strongest among them, Diocletian, instituted new military reforms. He recognized the grim reality that, sooner or later, attackers who were numerous and persistent enough would be able to penetrate the northern frontiers. So he stationed several small, mobile armies at strategic points along the borders. Their job was to move quickly, should the need arise, and intercept any invaders who made it past the Roman border defenses. One of Diocletian's successors, Constantine I, had these armies, each numbering about fifteen hundred men, move frequently from town to town, presenting a show of force all along the frontier.

This strategy worked well enough as long as invading troops were relatively few in numbers. By the 370s, however, more pressure than ever had built up behind the northern borders, and the proverbial dam finally broke, unleashing a mighty human torrent. In huge numbers, Vandals, Goths, Alani, Franks, and many others poured into Rome's northern provinces. One group, the Visigoths, delivered the emperor Valens a disastrous defeat at Adrianople, in northern Greece, in August 378. Valens died, along with some forty thousand Roman legionaries.

The defeat at Adrianople proved to be the beginning of the end for the Roman army. On the one hand, the government could not afford to recruit, equip, train, and maintain replacements for all of the lost troops. Also, the defeat was a serious blow to military morale. In the years that followed, it became increasingly difficult to find new recruits from the ranks of the Roman citizenry.

To make up for this shortfall, the government signed up more and more of the Germans who had settled in the northern provinces in recent years. Roman leaders saw that they were more than willing to fight other Germans in exchange for the right to settle in and become part of the empire. Modern historians often refer to this practice and policy as the "barbarization" of the Roman army. As it accelerated, it took a debilitating toll. Most of the "barbarian" troops fought under their own commanders. Also, the German warriors lacked discipline, effective organization, and respect for Roman values and tradition. In time, their lax attitudes and ways spread to most of the remaining citizen troops. Within two generations at most, the army was, for all intents and purposes, a barbarian, rather than a Roman, force.

The Army's Last Vestiges

In retrospect, it is clear that the decline of the Roman army could not have come at a worse time. Just as the military was experiencing a marked loss of quality and prestige and its ranks were filling with

The Huns invaded eastern Europe, driving local natives into Roman territories.

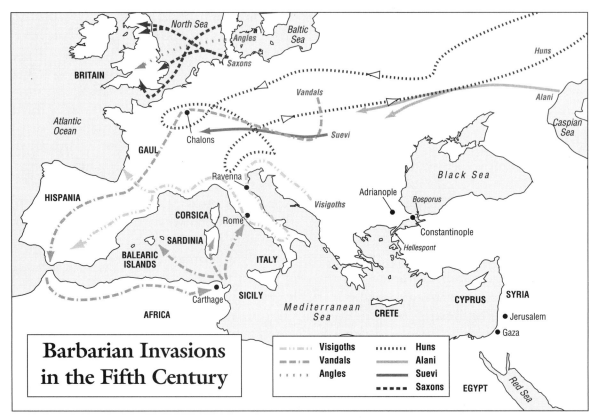

Barbarian Invasions in the Fifth Century

Germans and other non-Romans, the northern borders came increasingly under attack. The western part of the realm steadily shrank as the Vandals, Franks, Saxons, Angles, and others seized and settled in former Roman provinces.

Eventually, the western Roman government, which had for decades been ruled by weak or incompetent emperors, became irrelevant. The real power, or what was left of it, rested with the last of Rome's armies in Italy, a rough, motley, all-barbarian force. Its German-born commander, Odoacer, finally decided it was time to do away with pretenses. He demanded that the emperor, a young man named Romulus Augustulus,

step down from the throne. Then the German troops acclaimed Odoacer king of Italy, a territory that now constituted one of the last few remnants of the once great western Roman realm. Because no new emperor took the deposed Augustulus's place, these events have come to be seen as the official end of the western Roman Empire.

It was also the end of the Roman army. In its heyday, it had been the formidable instrument of power that had won Rome a vast empire. As that instrument had steadily weakened, so had the realm. And when the last, degraded vestiges of the army no longer cared to uphold and protect it, that realm could no longer survive.

Notes

Introduction: Empires Won by Force of Arms

1. Michael Grant, *The Army of the Caesars*. New York: M. Evans, 1974, p. xv.
2. Peter Connolly, *Greece and Rome at War*. London: Macdonald, 1998, p. 87.

Chapter 1: Rome's Early Enemies and Expansion

3. Michael Grant, *History of Rome*. New York: Scribner's, 1978, p. 47.
4. Livy, *The History of Rome from Its Foundation*, books 1–5 published as *Livy: The Early History of Rome*, trans. Aubrey de Sélincourt. New York: Penguin Books, 1960, p. 48.
5. Quoted in Livy, *Early History of Rome*, p. 58.
6. Livy, *Early History of Rome*, p. 61.
7. Livy, *Early History of Rome*, p. 81.
8. Livy, *Early History of Rome*, pp. 126–27.
9. Grant, *History of Rome*, p. 44.

Chapter 2: Undisputed Masters of Italy

10. Plutarch, *Life of Camillus*, in *Parallel Lives*, published complete as *Lives of the Noble Grecians and Romans*, trans. John Dryden. New York: Random House, 1932, p. 165.

11. Arthur E.R. Boak and William G. Sinnegin, *A History of Rome to 565 A.D.* New York: Macmillan, 1965, p. 51.
12. Plutarch, *Camillus*, p. 165.
13. Polybius, *The Histories*, published as *Polybius: The Rise of the Roman Empire*. Trans. Ian Scott-Kilvert. New York: Penguin Books, 1979.
14. Polybius, *Histories*, p. 130.

Chapter 3: Rome Against Carthage: Round One

15. Polybius, *Histories*, pp. 46–47.
16. Polybius, *Histories*, p. 62.
17. Polybius, *Histories*, p. 41.
18. Polybius, *Histories*, p. 54.
19. Polybius, *Histories*, pp. 50–51.
20. J.F. Lazenby, *The First Punic War: A Military History*. Stanford, CA: Stanford University Press, 1996, pp. 26–27.
21. Polybius, *Histories*, pp. 62–63.
22. Polybius, *Histories*, p. 63.
23. Polybius, *Histories*, p. 62.
24. Polybius, *Histories*, pp. 65–66.
25. Polybius, *Histories*, p. 81.

Chapter 4: Rome Against Carthage: Round Two

26. Grant, *History of Rome*, p. 98.
27. Chester G. Starr, *A History of the Ancient World*. New York: Oxford

University Press, 1991, p. 477.

28. Livy, *History of Rome*, books 21–30 published as *Livy: The War with Hannibal*, trans. Aubrey de Sélincourt. New York: Penguin Books, 1972, p. 26.

29. Livy, *The War with Hannibal*, pp. 60–61.

30. Livy, *The War with Hannibal*, p. 72.

31. Plutarch, *Life of Fabius*, in *Makers of Rome: Nine Lives by Plutarch*, trans. Ian Scott-Kilvert. New York: Penguin Books, 1965, p. 58.

32. Livy, *The War with Hannibal*, p. 149. Plutarch also reports Roman losses of about fifty thousand as does another Romanized Greek historian, Appian; by contrast, Polybius claims the Romans lost seventy thousand men at Cannae.

33. Livy, *The War with Hannibal*, p. 165.

34. Polybius, *Histories*, p. 477.

Chapter 5: Roman Armies Overrun Greece

35. Grant, *History of Rome*, p. 135.

36. Polybius, *Histories*, p. 509.

37. Polybius, *Histories*, pp. 511–12.

38. Livy, *History of Rome*, books published as *Livy: Rome and the Mediterranean*, trans. Henry Bettenson. New York: Penguin Books, 1976, pp. 256–57.

39. Grant, *History of Rome*, p. 140.

Chapter 6: Julius Caesar Conquers Gaul

40. Phillip A. Kildahl, *Caius Marius*.

New York: Twayne, 1968, p. 65.

41. Plutarch, *Life of Marius*, in *Fall of the Roman Republic: Six Lives by Plutarch*, trans. Rex Warner. New York: Penguin Books, 1972, p. 25.

42. Julius Caesar, *Commentary on the Gallic War*, in *War Commentaries of Caesar*, trans. Rex Warner. New York: New American Library, 1960, p. 23.

43. Caesar, *Gallic War*, pp. 47–48.

44. Plutarch, *Life of Caesar*, in *Fall of the Roman Republic*, pp. 259–60.

45. Grant, *Army of the Caesars*, p. 19.

46. Michael Grant, *Julius Caesar*. New York: M. Evans, 1992, p. 83.

Chapter 7: Rome's Early Imperial Conquests

47. Vegetius, *On the Roman, Military*, quoted in Grant, *Army of the Caesars*, p. xxvii.

48. Suetonius, *Lives of the Twelve Caesars*, published as *The Twelve Caesars*, trans. Robert Graves, rev. Michael Grant. New York: Penguin Books, 1979, p. 65.

49. Tacitus, *Agricola*, in *Tacitus: The Agricola and the Germania*, trans. Harold Mattingly, rev. S.A. Handford. New York: Penguin Books, 1970, p. 86.

50. Tacitus, *Agricola*, p. 86.

51. Tacitus, *Agricola*, p. 87.

52. Tacitus, *Agricola*, p. 88.

53. Tacitus, *Agricola*, p. 89.

Chronology

B.C.

753
This date (as computed and accepted by Roman scholars some centuries later) is the traditional founding date for the city of Rome by Romulus.

509
The leading Roman landowners throw out their last king and establish the Roman Republic.

496
The Romans defeat the other states of the Latin League at Lake Regillus.

431
Rome crushes the Volsci and Aequi, fierce Apennine hill peoples, at Mount Algidus.

396
The Romans capture the formidable Etruscan stronghold of Veii, twelve miles north of Rome.

390
At the Allia River, north of Rome, a Roman army is routed by an invading army of Gauls. Not long afterward, the Romans abandon the army's traditional phalanx and adopt manipular organization and tactics.

343
The first war against another hill people, the Samnites, begins.

340–338
Rome defeats the Latin League again and incorporates the territories of some of its members into the growing Roman state.

298–290
Rome fights and defeats the Samnites in the Third Samnite War.

280–275
The Romans fight several battles with the Greek Hellenistic king Pyrrhus, who has come to the aid of the Greek cities of southern Italy; his victories are so costly that he abandons the Italian Greeks to their fate.

265
Having gained control of the Italian Greek cities, Rome is master of the whole Italian peninsula.

264–241
The First Punic War, in which Rome defeats the maritime empire of Carthage, occurs.

225
The Romans defeat the Gauls in the Po Valley, in northern Italy, and take control of that region.

218–201

Rome fights Carthage again in the Second Punic War, during which the Carthaginian general Hannibal crosses the Alps, invades Italy, and delivers the Romans one crippling defeat after another.

200–197

The Romans defeat Macedonia in the Second Macedonian War.

190

A Roman army enters Asia Minor and defeats Antiochus III, king of the Seleucid Empire.

168

The Romans crush the Macedonian king Perseus at Pydna, in northern Greece, ending the Third Macedonian War.

149–146

Rome annihilates Carthage in the Third Punic War.

146

A Roman general razes the once great Greek city of Corinth to the ground as an example to other Greeks who might contemplate defying Rome.

118

The Romans establish a colony, Narbonne, in southern Gaul (now southern France).

107

Gaius Marius, a military general and war hero who will initiate significant army reforms, holds his first consulship.

58–51

Julius Caesar conquers the region of Transalpine Gaul (now central and northern France and Belgium), significantly expanding Roman dominion into Europe.

31

Octavian defeats Antony and Egypt's Queen Cleopatra at Actium (in western Greece) and gains firm control of the Mediterranean world. Soon, the Senate confers on him the title of Augustus, "the revered one," and he becomes, in effect, Rome's first emperor.

25

Roman armies enter the Alps in preparation for invading the Germanic lands beyond.

12

Drusus the Elder, stepson of Augustus, begins a three-year campaign in which he subdues much of central Germany.

A.D.
9

A Roman army of fifteen thousand men is annihilated in Germany's Teutoburg Forest, an event that forces Augustus to withdraw his forces from the German lands recently secured by Drusus.

43

A Roman army commanded by Aulus Plautius invades and rapidly subdues southern Britain.

84

The Roman general Agricola invades Caledonia (Scotland) and defeats the natives at Mons Graupius.

101
The emperor Trajan launches a campaign in Dacia, north of the Danube.

106
Trajan completes the conquest of Dacia and turns it into a new province.

117
Trajan dies; the Roman Empire has reached its greatest size and power.

235–284
The empire suffers under the strain of terrible political upheaval and civil strife, prompting later historians to call this period the Anarchy.

284
Diocletian ascends the throne and initiates sweeping political, economic, and social reforms, in effect reconstructing the empire under a new blueprint. (Modern historians often call this new realm the Later Empire.)

ca. 370
The Huns, a savage nomadic people from central Asia, sweep into eastern Europe, pushing the Goths and other "barbarian" peoples into the northern Roman provinces.

378
The eastern emperor Valens is disastrously defeated by the Visigoths at Adrianople (in northern Greece).

395
The last emperor to rule both western and eastern Rome, Theodosius, dies and leaves his young sons, Honorius and Arcadius, in charge of a divided realm.

ca. 407
As western Rome steadily loses control of several of its northern and western provinces, Britain falls under the sway of barbarian tribes.

410
Alaric, king of the Visigoths, briefly occupies and loots Rome.

455
The Vandals sack Rome.

476
The German-born general Odoacer demands that the emperor, the young Romulus Augustulus, step down. No new emperor takes his place, and the Roman Empire officially ceases to exist (though Rome and Italy remain prosperous for some time under barbarian rule). Meanwhile, the succession of Roman emperors continues in the eastern realm, which steadily evolves into the Byzantine Empire.

Glossary

as (plural *asses*): A copper coin worth one-fourth of a *sestertius*.

auxiliaries *(auxilia)*: Military forces, consisting of noncitizens recruited from the provinces, that supplemented the regular Roman legions during imperial times.

centuries: Small units within a Roman legion, at first containing one hundred men each and later containing eighty men each; a naval century consisted of the crew of one warship.

cohort *(cohors)*: A unit of a Roman army legion, usually consisting of about five hundred men, used in the late Republic and thereafter until Rome's last two centuries.

consul: In the Roman Republic, one of two jointly serving elected chief government administrators, who also commanded the armies; their office was the consulship, and matters pertaining to it or them were termed consular.

corvus: "Raven," or "crow"; a naval warfare device consisting of a wooden gangway with a spike protruding from the end, which stood upright on a Roman deck until dropped onto an enemy deck. The spike penetrated the deck and held the ships together while Roman soldiers ran across and boarded the other vessel.

cuirass: Chest armor.

denarius (plural *denarii*): A silver coin worth one twenty-fifth of an *aureas*.

equites: "Knights"; Roman businessmen and other well-to-do individuals who composed a non-land-based aristocracy second in prestige only to the landowning patricians; also, the cavalrymen drawn from this class.

garrison: A group of soldiers manning a fort or other installation.

gladius: The short sword wielded by Roman soldiers.

hastati: In Rome's mid-republican army, young soldiers who fought in the first line of infantry.

hoplite: A heavily armored infantry soldier who fought in the phalanx formation.

legion: An army battalion, consisting at first of about three thousand men, then about forty-two hundred, and later about five thousand or more.

legionary: An ordinary Roman soldier.

Liburnians *(liburnae)*: Small, fast, highly maneuverable warships used by the Romans, especially in their provincial fleets.

maniple: A tactical fighting unit, usually consisting of about 120 men, used in Rome's early and mid-republican armies.

manipular tactics: A basic combination of battlefield maneuvers in which the Roman maniples formed lines, each of which engaged in a separate charge against the enemy.

patricians: Landowners who made up Rome's wealthiest and most privileged class.

Pax Romana: "Roman Peace"; the highly peaceful and prosperous era initiated by Augustus, lasting from about 30 B.C. to about A.D. 180.

phalanx: A battle formation introduced by the Greeks and adopted by the early Romans. Ranks (lines) of infantry soldiers stood one behind the other, their upraised shields and thrusting spears creating a formidable barrier.

pilum (**plural** *pila*): A throwing spear (javelin).

principes: In Rome's mid-republican army, soldiers in the prime of their life, who fought in the second line of infantry.

quincunx: The pattern of dots displayed for the number five on a dice cube; also used to describe the checkerboard arrangement of the Roman maniples on the battlefield during republican times.

quinquereme: A warship likely having three banks of oars, with two men to an oar in the upper two banks and one man to an oar in the lowest bank.

scutum: A Roman legionary's originally oval and later rectangular shield. In the third century A.D., the *scutum* was abandoned as oval shields once more came into general use.

Senate: The Roman legislative branch, made up of well-to-do aristocrats. It directed foreign policy, advised the consuls, and in general controlled the state during the Republic.

sestertius (**plural** *sestertii* **or** *sesterces*): A silver or bronze coin originally equal to 2.5 *asses* and later to 4, and also .25 of a *denarius.*

standards: The emblems, flags, or colors of an army or army unit, usually raised on a pole as a rallying point for the soldiers.

triarii: In Rome's mid-republican army, older veterans who fought in the third line of infantry.

tribune (*tribunus*): "Tribal officer"; one of the six elected officers who ran an army legion; they ranked below a legate but above a centurion.

trireme: A warship having three banks of oars, with one man to each oar.

velites: In Rome's mid-republican army, light-armed skirmishers who threw javelins at the enemy and then retreated behind the infantry.

For Further Reading

Peter Connolly, *The Roman Army.* Westwood, NJ: Silver Burdette, 1979. A superb description of the ancient Roman military, well written, detailed, and beautifully illustrated, all by Connolly, one of the leading historians of ancient warfare. Highly recommended.

Phil R. Cox and Annabel Spenceley, *Who Were the Romans?* New York: EDC, 1994. An impressive, well-illustrated introduction to the Romans, presented in a question-and-answer format and aimed at basic readers.

Stephen Johnson and Jacqueline Morley, *A Roman Fort.* New York: Peter Bedrick, 2001. This informative little book contains several excellent color drawings reconstructing what a Roman fort looked like and how it was used.

Geraldine McCaughrean, *Roman Myths.* New York: Margaret McElderry (Macmillan), 2001. An extremely well-written introduction to Roman mythology for young people. The author's prose is enthusiastic and readable.

Don Nardo, *Life of a Roman Soldier.* San Diego: Lucent Books, 2001. A detailed yet easy-to-read volume summarizing life in the Roman army, including recruitment, training, camp life, armor, weapons, battle tactics, and more.

Judith Simpson, *Ancient Rome.* New York: Time-Life Books, 1997. One of the latest entries in Time-Life's library of picture books about the ancient world, this one is beautifully illustrated with attractive and appropriate photographs and paintings. The general but well-written text is aimed at intermediate readers.

Chester G. Starr, *The Ancient Romans.* New York: Oxford University Press, 1971. A clearly written survey of Roman history, featuring several interesting sidebars on such subjects as the Etruscans, Roman law, and the Roman army. It also contains many primary source quotes by Roman and Greek writers. For intermediate and advanced readers.

Major Works Consulted

Ancient Sources

Kenneth J. Atchity, ed., *The Classical Greek Reader.* New York: Oxford University Press, 1996.

Julius Caesar, *Commentary on the Gallic War*, in *War Commentaries of Caesar.* Trans. Rex Warner. New York: New American Library, 1960.

Dio Cassius, *Roman History: The Reign of Augustus.* Trans. Ian Scott-Kilvert New York: Penguin Books, 1987.

Dionysius of Halicarnassus, *Roman Antiquities.* 7 vols. Trans. Earnest Cary. Cambridge, MA: Harvard University Press, 1963.

Naphtali Lewis and Meyer Reinhold, eds., *Roman Civilization, Selected Readings.* Vol. 1. *The Republic and Augustan Age*; and *Roman Civilization, Selected Readings.* Vol. 2. *The Empire.* Both New York: Columbia University Press, 1990.

Livy, *The History of Rome from Its Foundation*, books 1–5 published as *Livy: The Early History of Rome.* Trans. Aubrey de Sélincourt. New York: Penguin Books, 1960; books 21–30 published as *Livy: The War with Hannibal.* Trans. Aubrey de Sélincourt. New York: Penguin Books, 1972; books 31–45 published as *Livy: Rome and the Mediterranean.* Trans. Henry Bettenson. New York: Penguin Books, 1976.

Cornelius Nepos, *The Great Generals of Foreign Nations.* Trans. John C. Rolfe. Cambridge, MA: Harvard University Press, 1960.

Plutarch, *Parallel Lives*, published complete as *Lives of the Noble Grecians and Romans.* Trans. John Dryden. New York: Random House, 1932; also excerpted in *The Age of Alexander: Nine Greek Lives by Plutarch.* Trans. Ian Scott-Kilvert. New York: Penguin Books, 1973; *Fall of the Roman Republic: Six Lives by Plutarch.* Trans. Rex Warner. New York: Penguin Books, 1972; and *Makers of Rome: Nine Lives by Plutarch.* Trans. Ian Scott-Kilvert. New York: Penguin Books, 1965.

Polybius, *The Histories*, published as *Polybius: The Rise of the Roman Empire.* Trans. Ian Scott-Kilvert. New York: Penguin Books, 1979.

Suetonius, *Lives of the Twelve Caesars*, published as *The Twelve Caesars.* Trans. Robert Graves, rev. Michael Grant. New York: Penguin Books, 1979.

Tacitus, *Agricola* and *Germania*, in *Tacitus: The Agricola and the Germania.* Trans. Harold Mattingly, rev. S.A. Handford. New York: Penguin Books, 1970.

———, *Annals*, published as *Tacitus: The Annals of Imperial Rome.* Trans. Michael Grant. New York: Penguin Books, 1989.

Modern Sources

Simon Anglim et al., *Fighting Techniques of the Ancient World, 3000 B.C.–A.D. 500: Equipment, Combat Skills, and Tactics.* New York: St. Martin's, 2002. The title describes the contents. Detailed and well written, with numerous full-color drawings by Peter Connolly, one of the great artistic interpreters of the ancient world. Highly recommended.

M.C. Bishop and J.C. Coulston, *Roman Military Equipment.* Princes Risborough, UK: Shire, 1989. A very useful summary of Roman arms and other military materials.

Averil Cameron, *The Later Roman Empire: A.D. 284–430.* Cambridge, MA: Harvard University Press, 1993. This well-written, somewhat scholarly volume contains excellent, generally up-to-date summaries of Diocletian's and Constantine's military and other reforms.

Lionel Casson, *The Ancient Mariners: Seafarers and Sea Fighters of the Mediterranean in Ancient Times.* Princeton, NJ: Princeton University Press, 1991. This enduring and popular book by a fine classical scholar contains several useful chapters on Roman ships, including warships. Casson includes a number of English translations of letters written by Roman sailors.

Peter Connolly, *Greece and Rome at War.* London: Macdonald, 1998. A highly informative and useful volume by one of the finest historians of ancient military affairs. Connolly, whose stunning paintings adorn this book and his others, is also the foremost modern illustrator of the ancient world. Highly recommended.

T.J. Cornell, *The Beginnings of Rome: Italy and Rome from the Bronze Age to the Punic Wars (c.1000–264 B.C.).* London: Routledge, 1995. A well-written, authoritative study of Rome's early centuries, including its conquests and military developments.

Arther Ferrill, *The Fall of the Roman Empire: The Military Explanation.* New York: Thames and Hudson, 1986. In this excellent work, written in a straightforward style, Ferrill supports the position that Rome fell mainly because its army grew increasingly less disciplined and formidable during the empire's last two centuries while at the same time the overall defensive strategy of the emperors was ill conceived and contributed to the ultimate fall.

Michael Grant, *The Army of the Caesars.* New York: M. Evans, 1974. A very informative volume that examines the evolving Roman army from the days of Marius in the late Republic to the much inferior Roman military machine of the Later Empire.

———, *The Fall of the Roman Empire.* New York: Macmillan, 1990. Grant here begins with a general historical sketch of Rome's last centuries and then proceeds with his main thesis, that Rome fell because of many manifestations of disunity, among them generals turning on the state, the poor versus the rich, the bureaucrats versus the people, the pagans versus the Christians, and so forth. An excellent resource filled with useful facts and interesting theories.

————, *History of Rome*. New York: Scribner's, 1978. Comprehensive, insightful, and well written, this is one of the best available general overviews of Roman civilization from its founding to its fall.

————, *Julius Caesar*. New York: M. Evans, 1992. A fine telling of Caesar's exploits and importance by one of the most prolific of classical historians.

Lawrence Keppie, *The Making of the Roman Army: From Republic to Empire*. New York: Barnes and Noble, 1984. Keppie, a noted scholar and archaeologist, begins with a fine overview of Rome's early military development, then goes into considerable detail on Roman soldiers, military equipment, and battles in the late Republic and Early Empire.

J.F. Lazenby, *The First Punic War: A Military History*. Stanford, CA: Stanford University Press, 1996. A first-rate overview of this important war.

John D. Montagu, *Battles of the Greek and Roman Worlds*. London: Greenhill Books, 2000. A useful compendium of the major Greco-Roman battles, in each case briefly summarizing the background, setting, combatants, tactics, and results.

Nicholas V. Sekunda et al., *Caesar's Legions: The Roman Soldier, 753 B.C. to 117 A.D.* London: Osprey, 2000. An excellent overview of the Roman evolving army, including manpower, organization, weapons, armor, and tactics.

Michael Simkins, *The Roman Army from Caesar to Trajan: An Illustrated Military History of the Roman Legions*. London: Osprey, 1984. The weapons, uniforms, camps, and battle tactics of Roman soldiers during the early empire are highlighted in this nicely illustrated volume.

Pat Southern and Karen R. Dixon, *The Late Roman Army*. New Haven, CT: Yale University Press, 1996. This well-written, scholarly volume examines the gradual, nearly three-century-long decline of the Roman army, beginning with the events of the "century of crisis" (the third century B.C.). Included are illuminating sections on weapons factories, fortifications, siege warfare, and troop morale.

G.R. Watson, *The Roman Soldier*. London: Thames and Hudson, 1969. One of the better of the many books on the Roman army, this one contains much detailed information about how the troops were recruited, their training, pay, weapons, camps, and so on.

Graham Webster, *The Roman Imperial Army*. Totowa, NJ: Barnes and Noble, 1985. A distinguished former University of Birmingham scholar, Webster delivers an information-packed study of the army as it evolved during the empire. Includes very useful chapters on frontier systems, camps and forts, and peaceful activities engaged in by the soldiers.

Terence Wise, *Armies of the Carthaginian Wars, 265–146 B.C.* London: Osprey, 1996. Another handsome and useful book in Osprey's series on ancient warfare, this one concentrates on the Roman military during the epic Punic Wars, in which Rome squared off against the powerful maritime empire of Carthage.

Additional Works Consulted

Lesley Adkins and Roy A. Adkins, *Handbook to Life in Ancient Rome*. New York: Facts On File, 1994.

Gavin de Beer, *Hannibal: Challenging Rome's Supremacy*. New York: Viking, 1969.

Arthur E.R. Boak and William G. Sinnegin, *A History of Rome to 565 A.D.* New York: Macmillan, 1965.

J.B. Bury, *History of the Later Roman Empire, 395–565*. 2 vols. New York: Dover, 1957.

Brian Caven, *The Punic Wars*. New York: Barnes and Noble, 1992.

Tim Cornell and John Matthews, *Atlas of the Roman World*. New York: Facts On File, 1982.

F.R. Cowell, *Cicero and the Roman Republic*. Baltimore: Penguin Books, 1967.

Michael Crawford, *The Roman Republic*. Cambridge, MA: Harvard University Press, 1992.

Roy W. Davies, *Service in the Roman Army*. Ed. David Breeze and Valerie A. Maxfield. New York: Columbia University Press, 1989.

John B. Firth, *Augustus Caesar and the Organization of the Empire of Rome*. Freeport, NY: Books for the Libraries, 1972.

Sir John Hackett, ed., *Warfare in the Ancient World*. New York: Facts On File, 1989.

P.A. Holder, *The Roman Army in Britain*. London: Batsford, 1982.

A.H.M. Jones, *The Later Roman Empire, 284–602*. 3 vols. Norman: University of Oklahoma Press, 1964.

Archer Jones, *The Art of War in the Western World*. New York: Oxford University Press, 1987.

Phillip A. Kildahl, *Caius Marius*. New York: Twayne, 1968. (*Note*: Kildahl's use of "Caius" is an acceptable variant of "Gaius.")

Edward N. Luttwak, *The Grand Strategy of the Roman Empire*. Baltimore: Johns Hopkins University Press, 1976.

Simon Macdowall, *Late Roman Infantrymen, 236–565 A.D.* London: Osprey, 1994.

E.W. Marsden, *Greek and Roman Artillery*. Oxford, UK: Clarendon, 1969.

Stewart Perowne, *The End of the Roman World*. New York: Thomas Y. Crowell, 1966.

Kurt Raaflaub and Nathan Rosenstein, eds., *War and Society in the Ancient and Medieval Worlds*. Cambridge, MA: Harvard University Press, 1999.

Justine Davis Randers-Pehrson, *Barbarians and Romans: The Birth Struggle of Europe, A.D. 400–700.* Norman: University of Oklahoma Press, 1983.

W.L. Rodgers, *Greek and Roman Naval Warfare.* Annapolis: Naval Institute Press, 1964.

Chris Scarre, *Chronicle of the Roman Emperors.* New York: Thames and Hudson, 1995.

Nicholas V. Sekunda, *The Roman Army, 200–104 B.C.* London: Osprey, 1996.

Michael Simkins, *Warriors of Rome: An Illustrated History of the Roman Legions.* London: Blandford, 1988.

Chester G. Starr, *A History of the Ancient World.* New York: Oxford University Press, 1991.

John Warry, *Warfare in the Classical World.* Norman: University of Oklahoma Press, 1995.

Index

Picture Credits

About the Author

Classical historian Don Nardo has published many volumes about ancient Roman history and culture, including *The Age of Augustus*, *A Travel Guide to Ancient Rome*, *Life of a Roman Gladiator*, and Greenhaven Press's massive *Encyclopedia of Greek and Roman Mythology*. Mr. Nardo also writes screenplays and teleplays and composes music. He lives in Massachusetts with his wife, Christine.